Coalition Military Operations
The Way Ahead Through Cooperability

Report of a French-German-UK-U.S. Working Group

April 2000

U.S.-CREST
Center for Research & Education
on Strategy & Technology
Arlington, VA

FRS
Fondation pour la Recherche
Stratégique
Paris

RUSI
Royal United Services Institute
for Defence Studies
London

SWP
Stiftung Wissenschaft und
Politik
Ebenhausen

The views expressed in this report reflect the deliberations of the members of a multinational working group, and are not necessarily those of their organizations or of any government. While the report represents a consensus view of the working group, individual members do not necessarily subscribe to every statement contained therein.

© U.S.-CREST 2000
ISBN 0-9629930-8-5
$14.95

Copies of this report in Acrobat (pdf) format may also be downloaded from the U.S.-CREST web site, at `http://www.uscrest.org/CMO.htm`

This publication may be quoted or reprinted without further permission, with credit to U.S.-CREST.

U.S. Center for Research and Education
on Strategy and Technology (U.S.-CREST)
1117 North 19th Street, Suite 1200
Arlington, VA 22209-1708
Tel: (703) 243-6908
Fax: (703) 243-7175
Email: uscrest@uscrest.org

TABLE OF CONTENTS

List of Figures and Tables v

List of Abbreviations vii

Introduction ix

Executive Summary xv

Note de Synthèse xix

Kurzfassung xxv

I. The International Security Environment 1
    Current and Emerging Risks 1
    Preparing for Coalition Military Operations 5
    Conclusion 9

II. Representative Mission Challenges 11
    Characteristics of the Representative Missions 11
    Required Operational Capabilities 13
    Maintaining Coalition Political and Military Cohesion .. 21
    Findings 26
    Development Objectives 26

III. Nature of Interoperability: Challenges for the Future .. 29
     New Dimensions of Interoperability and Cooperability .. 29
     Major Challenges 30
     Assessing the Value of Interoperability in Coalition Operations .. 33
     NATO Efforts and Activities to Enhance Allied Interoperability . 35
     Interoperability Successes and Issues 39
     Future Interoperability: Likely Risks, Improvements,
     and Impediments 41
     The Need for Empirical Experimentation 43
     Findings 44
     Development Objectives 45

IV. Technology: Opportunities and Concerns 47
    Technology Trends, Opportunities & Challenges 47
    Impact on Interoperability 49

	Impediments to Progress	50
	Findings	51
	Development Objectives	51
V.	**Organizational Issues**	53
	Why Examine Organizational Issues	53
	Organizational Experience and Practices	54
	The Limits of Traditional Approaches	55
	Organizational Forms and Characteristics	58
	Matching Form to Mission	60
	The Need for Exploratory Experimentation	60
	Findings	62
	Development Objectives	62
VI.	**Doctrine and Concept Development**	63
	What Doctrine Is	63
	Why Is Doctrine Important for Coalitions?	65
	How to Harmonize Doctrine	70
	Findings	73
	Development Objectives	74
VII.	**Conclusions and Recommendations**	77
	Conclusions	77
	Recommendations	79

Appendix A: On Decision-Making in Coalition 83

Appendix B: Extending Network-Centric Warfare to Coalition Crisis Management and Assessment 91

Appendix C: Experimentation Typology 101

Appendix D: Potential Coalition Experiments 107

Appendix E: Complexity 109

Appendix F: Joint Vision 2010 as a Conceptual Basis for Coalition Warfare and Operations of the Future 111

Appendix G: Glossary of Selected Terms 119

Appendix H: List of Working Group Members 121

LIST OF FIGURES AND TABLES

Figures

Figure 1: Spectrum of Coalition Military Operations 12

Figure 2: Levels of Interoperability 29

Figure 3: Mission Capability Packages 32

Figure 4: How Information Age Concepts Alter the Landscape 48

Figure 5: The Concepts/Operations Relationship 64

Tables

Table 1: Differences in Capability Requirements
across the Three Missions 22

LIST OF ABBREVIATIONS

ACCIS	Allied Command and Control Information System
ACTD	Advanced Concept Technology Demonstrations
C^2W	Command and control warfare
C^4ISR	Command, control, communications, computers, intelligence, surveillance, and reconnaissance
CBW	Chemical and biological weapons
CDE	Concept development and experimentation
CFBL	Combined Federated Battle Laboratory
CFSP	Common Foreign and Security Policy
CIP	Critical infrastructure protection
CIS	Communications and information systems
CJTF	Combined Joint Task Force
CONOPS	Concepts of operation
COTS	Commercial off-the-shelf
CWAN	Combined Wide Area Network
DCI	Defense Capabilities Initiative
DoD	United States Department of Defense
EU	European Union
FMB	Forward maintenance bases
GPS	Global Positioning System
IO	International organization
JAT	Joint Analysis Team
JTF	Joint Task Force
MCP	Mission Capability Package
MOOTW	Military operations other than war
NBC	Nuclear, biological and chemical weapons
NC^3A	NATO C^3 Agency
NGO	Non-governmental organization
OPSEC	Operations security
OSCE	Organization for Security and Cooperation in Europe
PVO	Private voluntary organization
RCOP	Relevant common operational picture
RMA	Revolution in military affairs
ROE	Rules of Engagement
SAB	Senior Advisory Board
WEU	West European Union

INTRODUCTION

PROJECT RATIONALE

Multinational military operations across virtually the entire spectrum of warfare have played an increasingly prominent role in international security policy since the end of the Cold War. The way in which the leading NATO allies pursue the transformation of their militaries, in terms of the adoption of new technologies, doctrine, and organizational structures, will play a central role in determining whether they can maintain the ability to operate effectively together in coalition military operations.

While discussing lessons learned from *Operation Allied Force* in Kosovo, U.S. Secretary of Defense William S. Cohen declared, "the notion...that the United States could have carried out this mission unilaterally is simply not true". This trend is likely to continue. Defense planners in each of the four countries represented in this project[1] expect that their governments will prefer in the future to undertake military operations in coalition rather than to act alone. By working with one another countries can more effectively protect national interests, promote stability, and respond to humanitarian needs. Acting together will increase the military and political weight of effort. Militarily, countries can combine their forces to increase overall strength. Politically, governments give their actions increased legitimacy by showing that states with often different perspectives agree on a particular goal.

NATO nations are attempting to incorporate rapidly moving information technologies into their military systems. However, the U.S. is pursuing this effort with greater resources than the European Allies, labeling it to be part of a "revolution in military affairs" (RMA). The question of how the major NATO powers can maximize interoperability given the radical military transformations that may take place in the next century is of critical importance.

The United States, France, and the United Kingdom have all made force projection the central organizing concept for their armed forces. The United Kingdom has already taken significant steps to reorient its forces toward force projection missions. The far-reaching defense reorganization that France announced in February 1996 is designed to enable the rapid projection of a 30,000 strong, sustainable force by the year 2002, thereby placing Paris in a position to make a major contribution to coalition military interventions. Germany continues to focus on collective conventional defense and, in parallel, has recently begun to strengthen crisis response capabilities and sustainability for peace support.

---

[1] A working group composed of individuals from France, Germany, the UK, and the U.S. carried out this project.

Coalition Military Operations: The Way Ahead Through Cooperability

There has been insufficient multinational dialogue within the transatlantic defense community on how the evolving incorporation of information technologies into military systems may affect the ability of NATO members to undertake coalition military operations. This project represents an attempt to foresee where the application of technology is likely to create coalition operational discontinuities and to recommend ways to overcome them.

The success of a coalition depends in large part upon the ability of its members to work effectively together. In the information age, this involves the ability to share information to achieve shared awareness and to synchronize efforts. Interoperability in its broadest context refers to the "ability to work together". However, over the years interoperability has become closely associated with hardware and software systems, such as the interchangeability of munitions or the ability of systems to exchange data. This has resulted in a tendency to ignore "higher levels" of interoperability, meaning those associated with the ability of organizations to work together. Participants in this project adopted the term "cooperability" to refer to and to focus attention upon these higher levels of interoperability, as well as upon the need to co-evolve organization, command concepts, and doctrine to take advantage of advances in technology that are making it easier for systems to exchange data.

OBJECTIVES

This study brings together a broad spectrum of expertise and opinion to examine how the four project countries can cooperate to harness information technologies and enhance coalition cohesiveness. Thus, the objectives of this quadripartite study have been to:

- assess the requirements for future coalition operations; and
- make recommendations to enhance cooperability and technical interoperability.

The project recommendations focus on technology development efforts, organizational concepts, and doctrine development that can maintain the ability of the major NATO military powers to undertake effective coalition operations while exploiting the information revolution to achieve gains in military capability. Implementation of the project recommendations would result in deeper cooperation in these areas among the four participating countries. Such cooperation could serve as well to accelerate change within the broader NATO framework. Overall, the project has also been a vehicle for communicating European views to U.S. defense planners as the U.S.

Introduction

Department of Defense (DoD) heads towards a new Quadrennial Defense Review, and to provide U.S. inputs into European defense planning.

METHODOLOGY

In 1998 the U.S. Center for Research and Education on Strategy and Technology (U.S.-CREST) recognized that the changing international security environment posed significant new challenges for coalition operations. It therefore proposed this project on future coalition military operations to the Royal United Services Institute (RUSI) in the UK, the Fondation pour la Recherche Stratégique (FRS) in France, and the Stiftung Wissenschaft und Politik (SWP) in Germany to seek their participation. The defense ministries in France, Germany, and the United Kingdom, and the U.S. DoD, all agreed to participate in the study in an advisory capacity. The bulk of the project's working group consisted of senior civilian and military officials from the three European defense ministries and the U.S. DoD, together with representatives from each of the research institutes. Advice from these defense officials largely shaped the contents of this report, which does not necessarily represent official views. Each country provided two senior representatives to act as a Senior Advisory Board (SAB) to the working group.

The project working group held a series of meetings between March 1999 and February 2000, having broken down this complex subject into five areas: threat, missions, technology, organization and doctrine. While there were inevitable overlaps between these areas, project participants believed that this would be the most feasible way to examine the issue of future coalition interoperability, as well as to facilitate creativity, issue identification and resolution. The project established sub-groups to examine these substantive areas in more depth.

Having served as a useful framework for analysis, these areas were synthesized into the following report structure. Chapter one looks at the international security environment, discussing current and emerging security challenges before considering models for multinational response. Chapter two on representative mission challenges characterizes three significant generic mission types and their required operational capabilities. Chapter three on future interoperability challenges introduces the nature of interoperability and cooperability, leading into more detailed discussion of technology, organization, and doctrine in chapters four through six. Chapter seven summarizes the working group's findings and recommendations.

The report appendices contain a number of working papers produced during the course of the project. Additional papers and other working group material can be found on the U.S.-CREST web site. Copies of this report in

Acrobat (pdf) format may also be downloaded from the U.S.-CREST web site, at `http://www.uscrest.org/CMO.htm`.

TERMINOLOGY

Before delving into the substance of the study, it is necessary to define a few key terms to ensure clarity and reduce the risk of confusion. One obvious term requiring definition is "coalition". The working group considered a coalition to be a group of states that chooses to act in concert with one another to achieve a specified goal or goals. Nevertheless, non-state actors, such as non-governmental organizations, relief agencies, local sub-state organizations, and companies will generally be present and will often be critical for mission success. Coalitions will therefore often have to develop effective mechanisms to deal with them.

In addition to the issue of non-state actors, this definition raises the issue of goals. The states in the coalition are those who choose to agree to expend resources to reach a particular goal. Observers often use the term "coalition of the willing" to describe such a group, although in the working group's view all coalitions consist of willing participants. Agreeing on the coalition's goal does not, however, mean that coalition members necessarily agree on the best means to achieve that goal. As discussed in chapters two and three, mission goals are one of several critical issues that can have a major impact on the coalition's cohesion.

This study is above all focused on coalition military operations that involve the four project countries as well as NATO's broader membership. NATO is of course an alliance that maintains a robust military structure as well as numerous organizations and agencies that seek to promote interoperability, and as such is extremely different from a "come as you are" ad hoc coalition. Nonetheless, the study uses the term coalition military operations for two reasons.

First, even when the types of missions considered in this study are conducted under NATO auspices, there are also likely to be non-NATO countries involved in these operations. Overall, these missions have significant ad hoc aspects that would not have been present in a Cold War Article V defense against the Warsaw Pact.

Secondly, countries participating in this project, as well as other NATO members, could become involved together in military operations that do not take place under NATO auspices, as was the case in the 1991 Gulf War and the humanitarian intervention in Somalia. Moreover, the European countries represented in this project may also lead a peace support or crisis management operation conducted under the auspices of the European Union in the future, with potential support from but no direct participation on the part of

Introduction

NATO or the United States. The term "coalition military operations" is meant to encompass all these various scenarios.

ACKNOWLEDGMENTS

The working group would like to thank a number of individuals who made particular contributions to its work. Judith Daly played an instrumental role in helping to launch the project. Jean-François Delpech chaired working group plenary sessions and SAB discussions, while David Alberts, Paul-Ivan de Saint-Germain, and Reinhard Vogt chaired the project sub-groups. David Alberts, Charles Barry, Yves Boyer, Michael Codner, Loup Francart, Dennis Gormley, Robert Grant, Richard Hayes, Joe Luquire, Xavier Pasco, Joachim Rohde, Michael Spirtas, Peter Stratmann, Edouard Valensi, and Uwe Wiemken all provided discussion papers and/or wrote sections of the working group report. Robert Grant and Michael Spirtas assured the overall management of the project as well as integrated the different contributions to the working group report into a single document. The working group would also like to thank the many European defense ministry and U.S. DoD officials who gave briefings on issues related to the project topic.

EXECUTIVE SUMMARY

STUDY OBJECTIVES AND METHODOLOGY

This study brought together a broad spectrum of expertise and opinion from France, Germany, the UK and the U.S. to examine how their countries can cooperate to harness information technologies and enhance coalition cohesiveness. Thus, the objectives of this quadripartite study were to assess the requirements for future coalition operations and to make recommendations to enhance cooperability and technical interoperability.

In order to carry out this study, the U.S. Center for Research and Education on Strategy and Technology (U.S.-CREST) solicited the participation of the Royal United Services Institute (RUSI) in the UK, the Fondation pour la Recherche Stratégique (FRS) in France, and the Stiftung Wissenschaft und Politik (SWP) in Germany. The defense ministries in France, Germany, and the United Kingdom, and the U.S. DoD, all agreed to participate in the study in an advisory capacity. The bulk of the project's working group consisted of senior civilian and military officials from the three European defense ministries and the U.S. DoD, together with representatives from each of the research institutes. The working group held a series of meetings between March 1999 and February 2000. Advice from the participating defense officials largely shaped the contents of this report, which does not necessarily represent official views.

THE IMPERATIVE OF COOPERABILITY

- Coalition operations need greater interoperability, and most importantly, a new focus on "cooperability", meaning the successful bridging between coalition partners of differences in doctrine, organization, concepts of operation, and culture.

- Coalition operations for peacekeeping, peace enforcement, and regional conflict have increasingly become the primary focus of military activity since the end of the Cold War.

- Preparation for undertaking coalition operations at the level of national governments, NATO, UN, OSCE, WEU/European Union, and other regional organizations represents a useful starting point, but there is still too exclusive an emphasis on technical interoperability, and not enough on cooperability.

- Formal alliances and large institutions are sometimes unlikely to generate progress fast enough to keep up with or take advantage of rapidly advancing technologies.

- Ad hoc processes and traditional coalition organizational approaches have "worked" to the extent required to enable coalitions to form and to carry out their military missions, but coalitions cannot continue to rely exclusively on them for four reasons.
  - First, coalition interventions are likely to face an increasingly difficult operating environment, across the full range of force projection missions.
  - Second, the technologies that enable command, control, communications, computers, intelligence, surveillance, and reconnaissance (C^4ISR) are advancing rapidly, creating enormous opportunities but also new risks for coalition operations.
  - Third, variable rates of technology exploitation on the part of Western militaries together with the influence of distinct national cultural approaches mean that countries are adapting doctrine, organization, and concepts of operation in different ways in order to leverage new capabilities.
  - Finally, the demands of modern military operations are rendering traditional coalition organizational solutions ineffective by themselves.

FINDINGS

- A need exists for exploratory experimentation in which promising approaches to coalition military operations are subjected to the rigors of war games, simulations, exercises, experiments and other environments where they can be evaluated by coalition partners.

- Undertaking a campaign of experimentation focused on coalition interoperability and cooperability would provide the participating governments, and the larger community of potential partners, with tangible measures and evidence of the benefits that can be expected from investments in technologies, interoperability, and cooperability.

- Taking advantage of existing laboratories, military educational institutions, networks, and currently planned experiments and exercises would permit initiation of a broadened effort with little added infrastructure cost.

- Each of the participating countries would need to contribute to defining the goals and specific experiments of the campaign.

- Decisive coalition action will depend on coalition partners reaching consensus on risk assessment.

- Much can be done regarding multinational risk assessment that does not involve exchanges of classified information.

- A better understanding is needed of the relationship between technology and asymmetrical threats, as well as of the risks associated with technology solutions to the problem of multi-level security.

- For most nations, coalition military operations as a functional area lacks adequate focus in the politico-military hierarchy.

- For lack of this focus, lessons learned frequently evaporate upon reassignment of the individuals charged with drawing them in the first place.

RECOMMENDATIONS

The recommendations below summarize the detailed development objectives found in each chapter, and they are applicable to all would-be coalition partners. Yet, it is the sense of the working group that the four nations represented in the study can, and should, form the nucleus through which the recommendations are implemented.

- Establish a multi-country analysis program on emerging security issues and establish data bases for the related contingencies. This program would operate in confidentiality, using open sources and unclassified information. The program's output would be selectively available for publication. The program would include several coordinated activities:
  - Assess the incorporation of extant and emerging technologies in asymmetric approaches to warfare.
  - Modeling of asymmetrical conflicts.
  - Develop a common methodology to assess the impact of threats and conduct analysis of alternative futures in the security environment as well as of their implications.
  - Undertake analysis of adversary intentions, including the use of asymmetric means.

- Undertake a vulnerability assessment of current and potential coalitions.
- Highlight hot spots that may call for coalition operations in the future.

* Establish experimental programs to explore new concepts and technologies for the purpose of co-evolving common enhancements to coalition operations for peacekeeping, peace enforcement, and regional conflict. A cooperative process among the participating countries would define the goals and individual experiments of the program. The program would:
  - Take as a starting point current NATO experience and capitalize on existing laboratories, networks, research and planned experiments and exercises.
  - Incorporate other nations and non-governmental organizations as the experimental setting dictates.
  - Begin with a high-level, multi-national table top wargame that includes red/blue war-gaming and role playing by coalition participants.
  - Focus initially on shared awareness and efficient, coherent coalition planning and execution.
  - Explore risk management approaches to information sharing and security.

* Establish focal points in each nation to serve as the nation's focus for cooperability/ interoperability. The focal points would:
  - improve the development and writing of allied joint ***doctrine***.
  - improve the allied joint ***training*** system.
  - improve the allied joint professional military ***education*** system.
  - establish a cooperative coalition ***lessons learned*** activity.
  - improve cooperation for ***C⁴ISR*** research, development and acquisition.
  - improve the support for the use of open-system ***architectures*** and commercial ***standards*** in solving cooperability and interoperability requirements.
  - evaluate new technology tools for improved crisis management and for addressing the risks of multi-level security.

NOTE DE SYNTHÈSE

OBJECTIFS ET MÉTHODOLOGIE

Cette étude, conduite par un groupe d'experts en provenance de France, d'Allemagne, d'Angleterre et des États-Unis, avait pour objectif d'examiner comment les nouvelles technologies de l'information, utilisées en coopération, permettaient d'améliorer la cohésion de futures opérations en coalition. A partir de l'analyse des conditions requises pour la conduite de telles opérations, le groupe quadripartite propose des mesures permettant d'améliorer la "coopérabilité" et l'interopérabilité technique.

A l'invitation de U.S.-CREST (U.S. Center for Research and Education on Strategy and Technology, États-Unis), le RUSI (Royal United Services Institute, Royaume Uni), la Fondation pour la Recherche Stratégique (FRS, France) et la Stiftung Wissenschaft und Politik (SWP, Allemagne) ont coopéré à cette étude. Les ministères de la Défense des quatre nations ont également accepté de participer à l'étude à titre consultatif. Le groupe de travail, composé de fonctionnaires civils et militaires de haut niveau et de représentants de chaque institut de recherche, a tenu une série de réunions entre mars 1999 et février 2000. Les avis des participants étatiques ont joué un rôle essentiel dans l'établissement de ce rapport, qui toutefois ne représente pas nécessairement des positions officielles.

LA COOPERABILITÉ, UN IMPÉRATIF

- Les opérations en coalition nécessitent une bonne interopérabilité des forces; cependant, il est nécessaire d'aller au-delà des aspects techniques et de porter une attention accrue à ce que le groupe appelle la "coopérabilité", c'est-à-dire à la compatibilité simultanée des doctrines, des organisations, des concepts d'emploi, des cultures militaires.

- Depuis la fin de la guerre froide, les opérations en coalition sont progressivement passées au centre des préoccupations, que ce soit pour le maintien ou pour l'imposition de la paix ou en cas de conflit régional.

- Leur préparation au niveau national et par des organismes internationaux tels que l'OTAN, l'OSCE, l'UE, l'UEO représente un point de départ nécessaire, mais l'accent est encore trop exclusivement mis sur l'interopérabilité technique, ignorant les problèmes pourtant essentiels de coopérabilité.

- Les alliances et les grandes institutions ne permettent pas toujours des progrès assez rapide pour tirer le meilleur parti de technologies elles-mêmes en évolution accélérée.

- Les mécanismes ad hoc et l'approche traditionnelle ont jusqu'à présent fonctionné de façon acceptable, en ce sens qu'ils ont permis de former des coalitions et de mener à bien leurs missions militaires, mais il ne sera plus possible dans l'avenir de reposer exclusivement sur de tels mécanismes pour les raisons suivantes:
  - Les interventions en coalition devront en général être envisagées dans des environnement opérationnels de plus en plus difficiles, recouvrant toute la gamme des missions de projection de force.
  - Les technologies de commandement, de contrôle, de communication, de traitement de l'information, du renseignement et des moyens de reconnaissance (C^4ISR) progressent très rapidement; cela suscite simultanément des opportunités considérables et des risques nouveaux pour les opérations en coalitions.
  - Du fait des écarts dans les rythmes d'adoption des technologies et des spécificités nationales, l'exploitation de ces nouvelles possibilités par les forces armées se fait de façon différente dans chaque pays, que ce soit pour les doctrines, les modes d'organisation ou les concepts opérationnels.
  - Étant donné les impératifs auxquels sont aujourd'hui soumises les opérations militaires, les solutions traditionnelles d'organisation des coalitions ne sont plus suffisantes.

CONSTATATIONS

- L'expérimentation commune permet aux participants d'évaluer les avantages et les inconvénients de différentes façons de concevoir des opérations en coalition; les idées les plus intéressantes devraient faire l'objet de jeux de guerre, de simulations, d'expérimentations, d'exercices.

- Un programme d'expérimentation axé sur les questions d'interopérabilité et de coopérabilité permettrait aux États participants, à leurs alliés et à leurs partenaires potentiels d'estimer avec précision les avantages de divers types d'investissements.

- Le coût supplémentaire d'un tel programme sera faible s'il fait systématiquement appel à des ressources déjà existantes ou en préparation: laboratoires, centres d'enseignement militaire, réseaux, expérimentations, exercices.

Note de Synthèse

- Chaque pays participant doit contribuer à définir les objectifs et les expériences spécifiques associés à ce programme d'expérimentation.

- Une action efficace en coalition n'est possible que si les partenaires sont suffisamment d'accord sur l'évaluation des risques.

- Dans une large mesure, l'évaluation multinationale des risques peut se faire à partir d'informations ouvertes, sans échange d'informations classifiées.

- Il est nécessaire de mieux apprécier la relation entre technologies et menaces asymétriques, ainsi que les risques associés à des solutions techniques apportées aux problèmes de confidentialité à plusieurs niveaux de sécurité.

- La spécificité des opérations militaires en coalition n'est pas suffisamment prise en compte dans la hiérarchie politico-militaire de la plupart des États.

- De ce fait, les enseignements tirés d'expériences ou d'exercices antérieurs ont souvent tendance à être assez rapidement oubliés, au fur et à mesure des réaffectations.

RECOMMANDATIONS

Les recommandations ci-dessous résument les objectifs de développement donnés en conclusion de chaque chapitre et sont applicables à tous les partenaires éventuels d'une coalition. Toutefois, le groupe de travail estime très souhaitable que les quatre nations ayant participé à cette étude soient au cœur de leur processus de mise en oeuvre.

- Créer conjointement un programme d'analyse des problèmes émergents de sécurité, incluant la constitution de bases de données pour les situations correspondantes. Bien que confidentiel, ce programme n'utiliserait que des informations de sources ouvertes non classifiées et ses conclusions pourraient dans certains cas être publiées. Il comprendrait entre autres les activités suivantes:
  - Évaluation de la prise en compte de technologies existantes et émergentes dans les conceptions asymétriques de l'art de la guerre.
  - Modélisation des conflits asymétriques.

- Développement d'une méthodologie commune pour évaluer l'impact des menaces et pour analyser des futurs possibles de l'environnement de sécurité et leurs implications.
- Analyse des intentions d'adversaires potentiels, y compris leur éventuelle utilisation de moyens asymétriques.
- Évaluation des vulnérabilités des coalitions présentes et futures.
- Mise en évidence et étude des points chauds qui peuvent nécessiter des interventions de coalition dans l'avenir.

- Établir des programmes conjoints d'expérimentation pour étudier de nouveaux concepts et de nouvelles technologies, dans le but de rendre plus efficaces les opérations en coalition pour le maintien et l'imposition de la paix et pour les conflits régionaux. Les objectifs et les expérimentations individuelles du programme seront définis conjointement. Ce programme devrait:
  - Prendre pour point de départ l'expérience présente de l'OTAN et tirer le meilleur parti des laboratoires, des réseaux, des travaux de recherche, des exercices et des expériences actuellement existant ou en préparation.
  - Inclure d'autres nations et des organisations non-gouvernementales, selon les besoins de l'expérimentation.
  - Débuter par un jeu de guerre multinational "sur table" avec des participants de haut niveau; il devrait inclure des jeux de rôle et représenter simultanément les coalisés et leurs adversaires.
  - Se concentrer initialement sur l'évaluation commune de la situation et sur la planification et l'exécution efficace et cohérente des opérations en coalition.
  - Explorer les méthodes de gestion des risques liés au partage de l'information et à la confidentialité à plusieurs niveaux de sécurité.

- Coordonner dans chaque pays le traitement des problèmes d'interopérabilité et de coopérabilité. Ces organes nationaux de coordination devraient avoir pour objectifs:
  - D'améliorer le développement et la rédaction des **doctrines** communes.
  - D'améliorer le système **d'entraînement** commun.
  - D'améliorer le système **d'éducation** professionnelle militaire commun.
  - D'établir une activité coopérative de recueil et d'archivage des **enseignements** dégagés par les coalisés.
  - D'améliorer la coopération en matière de recherche, de développement et d'acquisition de **C^{4}ISR**.

- D'améliorer le soutien à l'utilisation **d'architectures** ouvertes et de **standards** commerciaux pour la résolution des besoins de coopérabilité et d'interopérabilité.
- D'évaluer les nouveaux outils technologiques pour l'amélioration de la gestion des crises et pour l'évaluation et l'élimination des risques liés à la confidentialité à plusieurs niveaux de sécurité.

KURZFASSUNG

ZIELE DER STUDIE

Die vorliegende Studie erfaßt ein breites Spektrum von Fachwissen und Orientierungen aus Frankreich, Deutschland, dem Vereinigten Königreich und den Vereinigten Staaten, um zu untersuchen, wie diese vier Länder ihren Zusammenhalt bei künftigen Koalitionseinsätzen verbessern und dabei gemeinsam Fortschritte vor allem in der Informationstechnologie nutzen können. Es geht den Autoren darum, die dafür wichtigen Erfordernisse zu klären und Verbesserungen für Kooperationsfähigkeit und technische Interoperabilität zu empfehlen.

Für die Mitwirkung an diesem Studienvorhaben hat das U.S. Center for Research and Education on Strategy (U.S.-CREST), das Royal United Services Institute (RUSI) in Großbritannien, die Fondation pour la Recherche Stratégique (FRS) in Frankreich und die Stiftung Wissenschaft und Politik (SWP) in Deutschland gewonnen. Die Verteidigungsministerien aller vier Länder waren bereit, an dem Projekt beratend teilzunehmen. So bestand der überwiegende Teil seiner Arbeitsgruppen aus höheren Beamten und Offizieren dieser Ministerien sowie aus Repräsentanten der Forschungsinstitute. Die Gruppe traf in der Zeit zwischen März 1999 und Februar 2000 mehrfach zusammen. Stellungnahmen und Ratschläge der Teilnehmer aus den Ministerien und nachgeordneten Bereichen haben den Inhalt dieses Berichts, der nicht unbedingt offizielle Positionen wiedergibt, in hohem Maße geprägt.

DIE ZWINGENDE NOTWENDIGKEIT VON KOOPERATIONS- FÄHIGKEIT

- Koalitionseinsätze erfordern ein höheres Maß an Interoperabilität und, was am wichtigsten ist, eine Verlagerung des Hauptaugenmerks auf die "Kooperationsfähigkeit", d.h. die erfolgreiche Überbrückung von Unterschieden zwischen Koalitionspartnern in bezug auf Doktrin, Gliederung, Einsatzkonzepte und Kultur.

- Koalitionseinsätze im Rahmen von Friedenssicherung, Friedenserzwingung und regionalen Konflikten stehen seit dem Ende des Kalten Krieges zunehmend im Mittelpunkt militärischen Handelns.

- Ein sinnvoller Ausgangspunkt ist die Vorbereitung für Koalitionseinsätze auf Ebene der nationalen Regierungen, der NATO, der VN, der OSZE, der WEU/Europäischen Union und sonstiger regionaler Organisationen.

- Ad-hoc-Prozesse und traditionelle Ansätze für den Aufbau und die Gliederung von Koalitionen waren insoweit wirksam, als sie diese zustande brachten und ihnen ermöglichten, ihre militärischen Aufträge auszuführen. Indessen können sich heute Koalitionen aus vier Gründen nicht mehr ausschließlich auf solche Methoden stützen.
  - Erstens ist damit zu rechnen, daß Interventionen mit Koalitionen über die gesamte Bandbreite des potenziellen Einsatzspektrums unter zunehmend schwierigen Rahmenbedingungen erfolgen werden.
  - Zweitens entwickeln sich die Technologien, die für Führung, Fernmeldewesen, elektronische Datenverarbeitung sowie die Nachrichtengewinnung, Überwachung und Aufklärung (C^4ISR) wesentlich sind, rasch weiter, wodurch sich enorme Chancen, aber auch neue Risiken für Koalitionseinsätze ergeben.
  - Drittens führen ungleiche Fortschritte bei der Nutzung von Technologie in den westlichen Streitkräften zusammen mit dem Einfluß ausgeprägter nationaler kultureller Eigenheiten dazu, daß die Länder ihre Doktrinen, Gliederungen und Einsatzkonzeptionen in unterschiedlicher Weise anpassen, wenn es darum geht, neue Fähigkeiten zur Geltung zu bringen.
  - Und schließlich lassen bereits die veränderten Anforderungen zeitgemäßer militärischer Einsätze traditionelle Lösungen für Aufbau und Gliederung von Koalitionen unzureichend werden.

- Das Augenmerk liegt immer noch zu ausschließlich auf der technischen Interoperabilität und nicht in ausreichendem Maße auf der umfassenderen Fähigkeit zu Kooperation.

- Formelle Allianzen und große Institutionen sind manchmal kaum imstande, schnell genug Fortschritte zu erzielen, um mit rasch sich weiterentwickelnden Technologien Schritt zu halten oder von ihnen zu profitieren.

ERKENNTNISSE

- Es bedarf experimenteller Untersuchungen, in deren Verlauf erfolgversprechende Ansätze für militärische Einsätze im Koalitionsrahmen den harten Anforderungen von Planspielen, Simulationen, Übungen und anderen Verfahren unterworfen werden, um von den Koalitionspartnern beurteilt werden zu können.

Kurzfassung

- Die Durchführung eines Versuchsprogramms, das mit Schwerpunkt der Interoperabilität und Kooperationsfähigkeit zwischen Koalitionspartnern gilt, würde den beteiligten Regierungen und der größeren Gemeinschaft potenzieller Partner konkrete Anhaltspunkte und Belege für die Vorteile liefern, die als Ergebnis von Investitionen in diese Vorhaben und für sie relevante Technologien erwartet werden können.

- Die Nutzung vorhandener Laboratorien, militärischer Ausbildungseinrichtungen, Netzwerke und gegenwärtig geplanter Experimente sowie Übungen würde die Einleitung breiter angelegter Aktivitäten bei nur geringen zusätzlichen Infrastrukturkosten ermöglichen.

- Jedes der beteiligten Länder müßte dazu beitragen, die Ziele und konkreten Experimente des Programms zu definieren.

- Entschiedenes Handeln der Koalition wird davon abhängen, ob die Partner bei der Risikobewertung zu einem Konsens gelangen.

- Für die Aufgabe multinationaler Risikobewertung kann – auch ohne den Austausch von VS-Informationen - vieles errreicht werden.

- Es ist notwendig, die Zusammenhänge zwischen Technologieentwicklung und asymmetrischen Bedrohungen zu begreifen. Gleiches gilt für die Risiken, die mit technologischen Lösungen für den Umgang mit Daten verschiedener Geheimhaltungsstufen (multi-level security) verbunden sind.

- In der militärpolitischen Hierarchie der meisten Staaten wird der Problembereich Koalitionseinsätze funktional nicht angemessen berücksichtigt und abgedeckt.

- Ohne entsprechende Schwerpunktbildung gehen folglich häufig ausgewertete Erfahrungen verloren, sobald die individuell mit der Bearbeitung Betrauten versetzt werden.

EMPFEHLUNGEN

Die folgenden Empfehlungen fassen die in den einzelnen Kapiteln ausführlich dargestellten Entwicklungsziele zusammen. Und sie gelten für alle in Frage kommenden Koalitionspartner. Allerdings teilt die Arbeitsgruppe die Meinung, daß die vier im Rahmen dieser Studie vertretenen Staaten einen

Kern bilden können und sollten, mit dessen Hilfe diese Empfehlungen umgesetzt werden.

- Unter Beteiligung mehrerer Staaten sollte ein Programm zur Analyse sich abzeichnender sicherheitspolitischer Probleme eingerichtet werden. Auch sollte die Einrichtung von Datenbanken für die betreffenden Eventualfälle erfolgen. Dieses Programm würde vertraulich gehandhabt, aber primär offene Quellen und Informationen verarbeiten. Die Arbeitsergebnisse des Programms könnten selektiv zur Veröffentlichung zur Verfügung stehen. Das Programm könnte mehrere koordinierte Aktivitäten beinhalten:
  - Die Beurteilung der Einbeziehung sowohl vorhandener als auch sich entwickelnder Technologien in asymmetrische Formen der Kriegführung.
  - Die Darstellung asymmetrischer Konflikte in Form von Modellen.
  - Die Erarbeitung einer gemeinsamen Methodik zur Bewertung der Auswirkungen von Bedrohungen und die Durchführung von Analysen alternativer Zukunftsentwicklungen im sicherheitspolitischen Umfeld sowie deren Konsequenzen.
  - Die Durchführung der Analyse gegnerischer Absichten, einschließlich der Anwendung asymmetrischer Mittel.
  - Die Durchführung einer Beurteilung der Verwundbarkeit gegenwärtiger und potenzieller Koalitionen.
  - Die Erfassung von Krisenherden, die künftige Koalitionseinsätze erfordern könnten.

- Mit Hilfe von Experimentalprogrammen zur Untersuchung neuer Konzepte und Technologien sollen in einem abgestimmten Prozeß gemeinsame Verbesserungen für Einsätze von Koalitionen im Rahmen der Friedenssicherung, der Friedenserzwingung und regionaler Konflikte entwickelt werden. Die Ziele und die einzelnen Experimente eines solchen Programms würden von den beteiligten Staaten kooperativ definiert. Das Programm würde:
  - die aktuellen Erfahrungen der NATO als Ausgangspunkt nehmen und auf vorhandenen Laboratorien, Netzwerken, Forschungen sowie geplanten Experimenten und Übungen aufbauen.
  - andere Staaten und nichtstaatliche Organisationen einbeziehen, wie von der experimentellen Ausgangslage vorgegeben.
  - mit einem hochrangig besetzten multinationalen Planspiel (Rot/Blau) und entsprechenden Rollenspielen der Koalitionsteilnehmer beginnen.

- den Schwerpunkt zunächst auf gemeinsames Beurteilen der Lage und eine leistungsfähige, kohärente Planung der Koalition und ihre Umsetzung legen sowie.
- Risikomanagement-Denkansätze zur gemeinsamen Nutzung von Informationen sowie deren Sicherheit untersuchen.

- Einrichtung von Ansprechstellen in jedem Land, die jeweils als nationale Kernzelle für Fragen der Kooperationsfähigkeit/Interoperabilität dienen. Diese Ansprechstellen würden dazu beitragen,
    - die Erarbeitung und Abfassung alliierter streitkräftegemeinsamer **Führungs-** und **Einsatzgrundsätze** zu verbessern,
    - das alliierte streitkräftegemeinsame **Ausbildungswesen** zu verbessern,
    - das alliierte streitkräftegemeinsame **militärische Schulungswesen** für Berufssoldaten zu verbessern,
    - eine Stelle zur kooperativen Aufarbeitung der von der Koalition aus Erfahrung gewonnenen Einsichten ("**lessons learned**") einzurichten,
    - die Zusammenarbeit auf dem Gebiet der Forschung, Entwicklung und Beschaffung im Bereich der Führung, des Fernmeldewesens, der elektronischen Datenverarbeitung, der Nachrichtengewinnung, der Überwachung und der Aufklärung (**C⁴ISR**) zu verbessern,
    - die Unterstützung in bezug auf den Einsatz von offenen **Systemarchitekturen** und handelsüblichen **Standards** bei der Lösung von Anforderungen im Bereich der Kooperationsfähigkeit und Interoperabilität zu verbessern,
    - neue technologische Hilfsmittel für ein verbessertes Krisenmanagement und für die Risiken im Umgang mit Daten unterschiedlicher Geheimhaltungsstufen auszuwerten.

I. THE INTERNATIONAL SECURITY ENVIRONMENT

The post-Cold War international security environment is very diverse and unpredictable, as are the risks and challenges to coalition interests and forces that it contains. There is no single threat analysis methodology for the new world situation, and there are inherent advantages to varied examinations. It is clear that the further one attempts to look ahead, the greater the diversity and unpredictability of potential outcomes. It is tempting to look at near-term and long-term trends apart, but there is nonetheless a continuous, evolutionary process. Moreover, the time scales for particular trends are themselves often unpredictable, and new risks could and do emerge with unexpected rapidity.

A major element of the response to these more diverse and unpredictable challenges has involved preparing for coalition military operations to undertake new types of missions. A rapid and profound overhaul of the Atlantic Alliance has taken place during the 1990's, reflected in the frequent holding of summit meetings. After its first version in 1950, the Alliance's Strategic Concept was revised only twice during the Cold War period. Two major revisions have occurred in less than ten years, in 1991 and 1999. Such activism reflected the need for the Alliance to adjust to the changed security environment, but also, since the mid 1990's, to the European goal of developing its own defense capabilities in the framework of the nascent European Union (EU). Both the adaptation of the Atlantic Alliance and the development of European defense capabilities have focused on the need to have a greater ability to conduct coalition force projection operations in order to meet the challenges of the post-Cold War security environment. These force projection operations can help provide for greater stability in Europe and the surrounding geographic areas.

CURRENT AND EMERGING RISKS

Significant sources of instability and conflict will continue to exist, and potentially grow, both in Europe and around the globe. These sources of instability include expanding populations containing a large proportion of disaffected youth; ethnic, racial, and religious tensions; competition for resources such as water, oil, food, and strategic metals; and the increasing power of non-state actors. Many disaffected youth are ending up in urban environments. The distinction between political or criminal motivation behind non-state risks is becoming increasingly blurred, as terrorist groups, drug traffickers, and other criminal elements have been establishing strong links with each other.

Many sources of instability are domestic in nature, but due to globalization the conflicts that result from them may affect large numbers of other states. Foreign adventures as a response to internal difficulties have been a long-standing phenomenon. Moreover, domestic strife can often spill over into neighboring states and regions. Refugees and economic migrants will be an increasing by-product of such problems. Foreboding demographic, economic, and environmental trends all mean that "failed states" are likely to remain an important feature of the future international security environment. These states suffer from a severe breakdown of governmental authority, and are unable to provide for the basic needs of a substantial element of their population. Somalia constitutes a leading example of a failed state. The erosion of the authority and autonomy of the nation state appears to be an enduring phenomenon, with implications both for the origins of conflicts and the way in which governments can respond to them.

The reemergence of a global peer competitor to the United States is unlikely before 2015 and probably beyond. Nonetheless, a number of countries, above all China, hold the potential to greatly increase their strategic and military reaches over the next several decades. Regional peer competitors could also emerge. These regional peers would not present problems of a global nature, but could have the potential to mount major challenges in niche areas of military capability or within their own geographic sphere. Regional competitors whose regimes operate outside the bounds of international norms (possibly combining hostility to the regional status quo, attempted acquisition of nuclear, biological, and chemical (NBC) weapons, and support for terrorist and criminal activity) will arguably present the most serious challenges to the interests of democratic nations in the absence of a global peer challenger.

New applications of warfare will further complicate the future security environment. Potential adversaries will not be able to match Western countries in terms of conventional military capability, and are likely to resort to asymmetric responses and operations. NBC weapons and corresponding delivery systems, terrorism, and cyber warfare constitute three leading instruments of asymmetric response. Adversaries will attempt to draw civilians into the conflict in order to capitalize on the reluctance of democratic nations to inflict civilian casualties and collateral damage, as illustrated in the recent war in Kosovo.

The rapid spread in coming years of technology that has civilian as well as military uses will help feed this likely resort to asymmetric responses and operations. In the near to medium term, the most significant risk to deployed forces is likely to come from the use of NBC weapons. While the number of new nuclear states may increase only slightly, chemical and biological weapons (CBW) programs are seeing broader success due to continued proliferation of pertinent equipment, technology, and knowledge with both weapons and commercial applications. CBW is of increasing concern both as an instrument of terror as well as a means of inhibiting or denying military operations. The latter would include access denial via attacks on embarkation points and staging areas as well as direct attacks on deployed forces.

With military forces increasingly exploiting commercially available technologies and equipment, these capabilities will, by definition, be available to non-military actors. Such groups may be organizationally and doctrinally better able to adapt new methods, technologies, and systems than Western militaries. Moreover, the means employed by sub-state and non-state groups will be varied and subject to other proliferation venues and technological sophistication.

As information technology becomes ubiquitous in military and commercial applications, efforts to conduct information warfare through attacks and manipulation of an opponent's information systems and infrastructure will become an increasingly important part of warfare. Democratic, open societies are vulnerable to information warfare and such operations could be used to disrupt allied cohesion. Advancements in cryptography may become a key tool for fighting in the information age.

High-resolution space imagery is available at low cost, giving both state and non-state actors access to information that not long ago was the sole purview of the superpowers. Utilization of "military" quality imagery would also include self-examination in order to improve upon denial and deception. Cellular communications and laptop computers can form the core of a robust, mobile command and control system for military operations that has high redundancy. Such a command and control system can allow, for example, dispersed, concealed militia type units more effectively to seize opportunities to mass for the purpose of achieving local advantage.

Other advanced military technologies are also likely to proliferate. Deployed forces in the future could come up against not only NBC weapons delivered via ballistic and cruise missiles, but advanced sensor capabilities, sophisticated air-defense weapons within integrated systems, and information warfare techniques. In the future, Somali-type "technicals" might possess SA-18's and laser-guided mortars shells in addition to more traditional AK-47's. Serb forces might be able to fire ground-launched cruise missiles using GPS guidance and armed with chemical or biological warheads.

This multifaceted technology proliferation is facilitating the development of "hybrid" militaries. These militaries, which cause particular concern, are organized around industrial era platforms with selected state-of-the-art niche capabilities. Hybrid militaries could present a particularly serious challenge within their own region. In many of these "aged" platforms, selected subsystems such as advanced fire control systems and improved avionics will have been installed, potentially improving operational capabilities. For many, this will be a cost-effective means of spending limited defense resources while extending the battlefield utility of aging and obsolescent weapons platforms. India is upgrading its aging MiG-21 fighters to cover air force shortfalls, China has mounted an advanced Israeli Phalcon radar on a Soviet vintage transport, and the Ukraine has developed a lucrative business by modernizing dated Soviet tanks.

Overall, the ability of many states to deter, prevent, or degrade outside intervention is increasing through the acquisition of sophisticated land, air, and sea denial capabilities. Land and sea mines fall into this category. Tactically, defensive weaponry can provide operational freedom that permits strategically offensive policies. The proliferation of coastal and air defenses is a source of particular concern. Regional state and non-state actors may also concentrate on attacking the more vulnerable "tail" rather than the stronger "teeth" of a coalition intervention force. Democratic societies themselves may increasingly become the target of various forms of attack that are meant to impose unacceptably high costs as the price of intervention. The support and exploitation of terrorist and criminal groups by state governments is not a new concept, and is likely to endure as an asymmetric response to conventional superiority.

Large-scale urban areas will provide fertile breeding grounds for terrorist and criminal groups in their search for new recruits, as well as a complex zone for future conflict. The challenge to future coalition operations from large-scale urban areas comes not merely from the concentration of people but also from the inability of infrastructures to handle the larger numbers. By the year 2000 the world contained more than 400 cities having over one million inhabitants, with 260 of these cities located in the developing world. By 2020 over half of the world's population will live in urban centers. Civil infrastructures are already stressed, a condition that will be further exacerbated over the next two decades. This type of security environment will be difficult to manage due to the risk to civilians as well as to the limited adequacy of high-tech solutions, such as sensor systems and stand-off precision weapons.

Looking over a very long-term period, there is the distinct possibility that as we move into the third decade of the next century a new peer competitor may have arisen. It may not be a single state, and indeed, could very well be an alliance. There is the possibility that it could also involve one or more supranational entities or groups.

The nature and dynamics of knowledge acquisition, global economics, and political dispositions may be totally reshaped by 2030. Through continued advancements primarily in biotechnology, micro-technology, and information technology, nations, groups, and individuals will have enormous potential for both good and ill-will. Key technological innovations with potential military applications include new bio-mechanical manufacturing processes using tools of bioengineering to produce molecular scale mechanical systems at low cost. By the end of the second decade of the 21st century, radically different tools for military conflict will begin to develop, particularly from the merger of applied bio-, micro- and nano-technology.

PREPARING FOR COALITION MILITARY OPERATIONS

NATO Adaptation

NATO's 1991 revision of its Strategic Concept already recognized that the Alliance had to move beyond collective defense and take into account a broader range of missions in order to remain relevant to transatlantic security. The 1999 Strategic Concept, released at NATO's fiftieth anniversary summit in Washington DC, took this idea further, explicitly committing the Alliance to "stand ready, case-by-case and by consensus... to contribute to effective conflict prevention and to engage actively in crisis management, including crisis response operations".

Between the release of the two Strategic Concepts, NATO adopted the combined joint task force (CJTF) concept. Although deployable in Article V operations, the creation of CJTF's responded above all to NATO's need to have enhanced capabilities for contingency interventions. The concept is designed to satisfy a critical interplay of operational and political objectives, providing substantial flexibility in both respects. Operationally, CJTF's feature short reaction time, deployability, and modular composition and augmentation by drawing on other headquarters and forces. Politically, CJTF's can be configured for a NATO- or a European-led intervention that uses NATO military assets. Either of these options can also include non-NATO or non-EU partner nations. Thus, strategic commanders and nations will configure the combined, joint force and the augmented CJTF headquarters on a case-by-case basis.

CJTF's cannot succeed unless sufficient reaction forces are available with the necessary operational capabilities. At its fiftieth anniversary summit NATO also formally launched the Defense Capabilities Initiative (DCI), which is explicitly designed to adapt the military forces of NATO nations to meet new risks and missions. The DCI emerged from NATO's November 1998 conference in Norfolk on "Transforming NATO to Meet the Challenges of the 21st Century". The goal of the initiative is to identify shortfalls in military capabilities, above all for force projection operations, and to provide a new mechanism for addressing those shortfalls. The DCI also places strong emphasis on making headquarters and forces interoperable. The DCI identified five areas of capability shortfalls:

- deployability and mobility,
- sustainability and logistics,
- effective engagement,
- survivability of forces and infrastructure, and
- NATO C²I systems

For each deficiency area, the DCI formulated near-term as well as longer-term projects. The DCI represents an important effort to fill in critical gaps in operational capabilities. However, the large number of projects formulated under the DCI will inevitably require nations to establish priorities for addressing the most urgent and significant shortfalls. Although a NATO initiative, the DCI is highly relevant as well for the EU's effort to enhance its own defense capabilitie's.

Implementing the European Union's Security and Defense Policy

The new dynamic generated by the 1991 Maastricht Treaty not only transformed the European Economic Community into a political union but also aimed at developing, within the framework of the Union, a common foreign and security policy (CFSP). This goal was agreed as well by the allies at the Berlin summit in 1994 when NATO accepted the development of a "European Security and Defense Identity" (ESDI). Most of the 1990's were, however, clouded with uncertainties and ambiguities about the EU's CFSP, in particular with respect to its relationship with NATO. The situation was radically transformed when France and Britain agreed at Saint-Malo in December 1998 to give impetus to the setting up of a European defense policy.

In the Saint-Malo declaration, the two countries agreed that "the Union must have the capacity for autonomous action, backed by credible military forces, the means to decide to use them, and a readiness to do so, in order to respond to international crisis". The declaration added that the EU must acquire appropriate structures and capabilities for analyzing crisis situations, intelligence assets, and a capability for relevant strategic planning, without unnecessary duplication, taking into account the existing assets of Western European Union (WEU). Chancellor Schroeder also subsequently acknowledged this dynamic. At the 73rd Franco-German bilateral meeting in Toulouse in May 1999, Germany and France expressed their determination to use all their weight to push for EU acquisition of the means needed to decide and deal autonomously with crises.

European leaders at the EU Cologne summit meeting in June 1999 used wording similar to that of the Saint-Malo declaration in asserting that the EU would play its full role on the international stage. To that end, they expressed their intent to give the EU the necessary means and capabilities to assume its

The International Security Environment

responsibilities regarding a common European policy on security and defense, including the capacity for autonomous action, backed by credible forces and the means to decide to use them.

Such agreement on the substance of ESDI led the 15 EU member nations to reflect on the general lines of an institutional architecture that would allow the European Council to take decisions about military actions related to humanitarian intervention, peace support operations, and crisis management. This architecture, inspired by the NATO machinery in its broad outlines, was agreed upon at the EU's Helsinki summit of December 1999. This agreement lays the foundation for the EU to have the autonomous capacity to take decisions and, where the Alliance as a whole is not engaged, to launch and then to conduct EU-led military operations. These operations are related to crisis management tasks, and could involve forces up to the size of an army corps (50,000 to 60,000 personnel), with its associated command, air and maritime support.

At a time of unprecedented budgetary constraints, this new impetus behind ESDI has also increasingly led France, Germany and the UK to reflect on the combined technical efforts necessary to set up a reasonable, common European military capability. Such an effort has been underway for several years in selected areas that bring both a strategic dimension to European cooperation and decisive operational control for potential limited regional conflicts.

For example, France, Germany and the UK have pursued continuous contacts on the subject of space telecommunications, through the Trimilsatcom program, even if national difficulties and differences in approach have stalled these cooperative endeavors. According to the French Government, the recent administrative arrangement between Germany and France for sharing some future Satcom capabilities lays the groundwork for closer cooperation in preparing next steps in this field.[2] It can also provide Europe with supplementary means to be part of the future choices of the Alliance regarding the strengthening of interoperability. On the British side, existing national capabilities with the Skynet satellite series can help Europe to envisage a future complete satellite communications system, both adapted to its needs and fully interoperable with Alliance assets.

In the same vein, Europeans have undertaken a small but enduring effort in the satellite data collection area, with the launch of the Helios 1A satellite in 1995, and the recent launch of a second Helios 1B reconnaissance satellite

---

[2] Press Briefing, Franco-German Cooperation in the Domain of Telecommunication Satellites, 30 November 1999, Directorate for Defense Information and Communication, French Ministry of Defense. Other countries, such as Belgium and the Netherlands, have officially stated their interest for such future arrangements in the Satcom field.

in December 1999. This effort is organized on a multinational basis with a fair degree of success.[3]

These efforts are certainly not enough. The European countries have reached a high level consensus regarding the need to develop sufficient strategic capability both to allow them to carry out operations in a number of possible war-fighting scenarios, and to assume their fair share in coalition military actions alongside their North American allies. In this regard, the lessons drawn from the recent Kosovo conflict should certainly act as a driver for the European countries today and lead them to overhaul their capabilities in a number of identified strategic areas. It is a necessity for Europe itself but also for the Alliance to build a genuine and reliable partnership. In this respect, it suffices to mention current shortcomings in the field of common intelligence capabilities, which require better optical and radar assets, especially where complementary national resources could be developed, and the need for more coherent approaches and procedures for data handling and sharing once they are collected.

A great deal of commonality between the strategic interests, needs and capabilities of the EU members, and particularly of Germany, France and the United Kingdom, put these perspectives in a naturally favorable climate. From a pragmatic point of view, it is certainly desirable to use these common national postures as a factor of efficiency for improving the interoperability aspects of coalition warfare. In this regard, it was agreed during the British-French summit of 25 November 1999, that the countries would make available the UK's Permanent Joint Headquarters and France's *Centre Operationnel Interarmées* and their planning capabilities as options to command EU-led operations. As part of this, France and the UK expressed the intent to develop standing arrangements for setting up multinational cells within these headquarters, including officers from other EU partners. In addition, Germany offered the German Army Forces Command and the Maritime Headquarters as operational headquarters to command EU-led operations. A European approach in this area is well at hand, paving the way towards broader and well-structured allied interoperability.

Thus, further thought on the means needed to make Europe fully able to respond on its own to crisis situations, alongside the deliberations conducted within NATO, must be seen as a decisive process in the building of a large and interoperable allied coalition force. Based on these guidelines, this pragmatism is precisely what can lead the European nations to consider NATO developments as logical and realistic steps in the common quest for

---

[3] According to recent military personnel declarations, the "common use planning" of Helios imagery by the three contributing countries (France, Italy and Spain) reached 17% for the last six months of 1999 and should total 25 to 30% by the end of 2000.

technical and operational coherence. In this perspective, the DCI may play a very important role.

Other International Security Structures
Security situations outside of Europe and indeed around the world have called for an organized response beyond that of NATO and the ESDI. These may be carried out through the auspices of the UN or of regional organizations such as the African Crisis Response Initiative and the Association of Southeast Asian Nations. The UN is seeking to develop a more effective crisis response capability, and regional organizations are likely to proliferate as well as develop both greater cohesion and military capability. They will therefore become increasingly important, perhaps even dominant, factors in future operations. It is possible to envisage varying levels of interventions depending on the cohesion and effectiveness of a regional security organization. Thus, outside countries' or coalitions' involvement may range from providing enablers such as transport or intelligence to fully functioning regional organizations, to undertaking a full-fledged intervention to prop up or replace the local force. In any case, it will be important to understand regional organizations, and ideally to influence their development in order to facilitate future cooperation.

CONCLUSION

Current and emerging security risks are driving the need for new force projection missions (discussed in the next chapter). They also determine the operational capabilities that countries require in order to carry out these missions. Significantly, working group members from four different countries agreed on the characterization of security risks contained in this chapter. NATO, the EU, other regional security organizations, and the UN all provide models for coalition force projection operations. The working group's analyses, findings and recommendations are most immediately relevant to the NATO and EU models, but could also be applied to other venues.

II. REPRESENTATIVE MISSION CHALLENGES

National interests and values have led democratic nations to undertake a significant number of military interventions since the end of the Cold War. Study group members agreed that peacekeeping, peace enforcement, and regional conflict will constitute the bulk of the demand for coalition operations out to 2015. Consequently, the study group decided that these mission areas should constitute the primary scenarios used to drive out interoperability problems. The study group also decided that each mission scenario would require the deployment of forces over a considerable distance, in order to make the scenarios as stressful as possible. Examples used for each type of scenario were Cyprus for peacekeeping, Bosnia for peace enforcement, and the 1991 Gulf War for regional conflict.

CHARACTERISTICS OF THE REPRESENTATIVE MISSIONS

The study group developed the following set of assumptions for each generic mission scenario:

Peacekeeping
- UN/OSCE mandate
- Coalition of the willing
- Permissive operation
- Impartiality
- Extended operation
- Need for political exit strategy/end state

Peace enforcement
- UN/OSCE mandate
- Coalition of the willing
- Tiered coalition (some coalition partners operate in front-line combat role while others lack either a mandate or the necessary capabilities)
- Non-permissive environment
- Extended operation
- End state (control and stabilize)

Regional conflict
- Intervening coalition of the willing is a party to the conflict
- Mandate possible but not essential
- Coalition of the willing
- High intensity conflict - decisive result sought
- Risk of escalation
- Clear end state

In broad terms, peacekeeping and peace enforcement are types of operations that seek to control violence. The intervening coalition does not have the goal of defeating an identified adversary, but rather of creating an environment in which political reconciliation between the belligerent parties in the theater can take place. Military responsibilities will primarily concern preventing, controlling, and stopping the use of violence, in particular against the civilian population. In regional conflict, on the other hand, the intervening coalition seeks to impose its will on an aggressor state, with military victory constituting the primary means of achieving this objective. While peacekeeping operations are based upon the consent of the belligerent parties, only limited initial consent characterizes peace enforcement missions. In both cases, however, the intervention force must possess sufficient operational credibility to carry out its mission. Figure 1 depicts this typology.

Figure 1: Spectrum of Coalition Military Operations

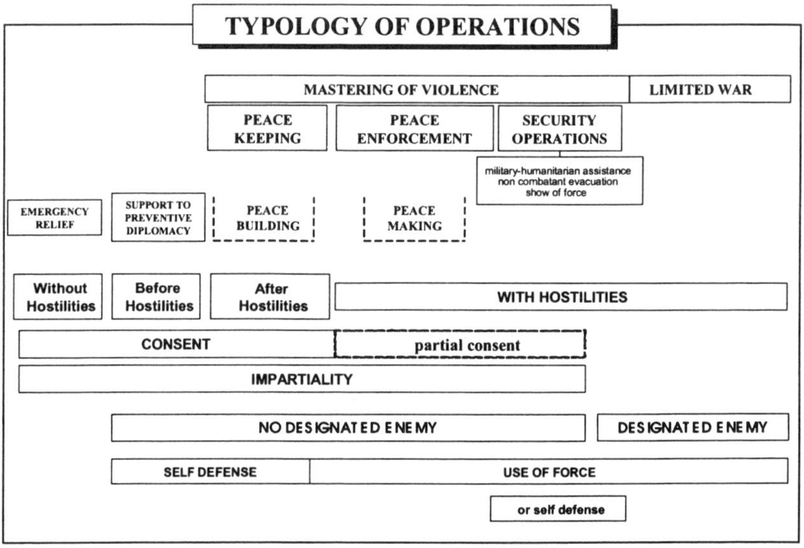

TYPOLOGY OF OPERATIONS					
		MASTERING OF VIOLENCE			LIMITED WAR
		PEACE KEEPING	PEACE ENFORCEMENT	SECURITY OPERATIONS	
				military-humanitarian assistance, non combatant evacuation, show of force	
EMERGENCY RELIEF	SUPPORT TO PREVENTIVE DIPLOMACY	PEACE BUILDING	PEACE MAKING		
Without Hostilities	Before Hostilities	After Hostilities	WITH HOSTILITIES		
	CONSENT		partial consent		
	IMPARTIALITY				
	NO DESIGNATED ENEMY			DESIGNATED ENEMY	
	SELF DEFENSE		USE OF FORCE		
			or self defense		

For the next 10 to 15 years, the international security environment will be replete with situations that will fall short of major war yet warrant attention by the international community. The threat from hybrid militaries in regional conflict is arguably the most significant one that coalition militaries will confront in the absence of a peer competitor. However, future scenarios that are further down in the security spectrum will occur with far greater frequency. Simultaneous contingencies are a real possibility and will exacerbate interoperability problems. Challenges to interoperability within peace support operations will often be primarily in the diplomatic and political arena, while military interoperability in general will be stressed as the situation approaches the regional conflict scenario. Technology will play an ever increasing part in establishing sufficient interoperability within coalitions and alliances. Conversely, overdependency on advanced technology can prove detrimental and produce vulnerabilities. Many challenges will be systemic across all phases of military operations in each of the three major contingencies, varying only in intensity and scope.

If global trends in force downsizing and restructuring continue, then countries should be able to maintain readiness. If, however, sufficient funds are not allocated for training, modernization, and personnel, then even force readiness for peacekeeping operations could become problematic. Multiple and simultaneous contingencies will stress not just the coalition itself but the feasibility of creating a coalition. The stress will be across capabilities but probably most notable in the ability to project and sustain forces.

REQUIRED OPERATIONAL CAPABILITIES

The tasks and implied capabilities associated with the three missions can be grouped under the broad headings of provision of command and control arrangements, intelligence and information, deployment and mobility, conduct of operations, and protection and sustainment.[4] For the purposes of this study, the focus is on capabilities at the operational and tactical levels. However, strategic aspects of mobility, intelligence and information also bear mentioning.

Provision of Command Arrangements

The essential tasks associated with the provision of command arrangements include provision of information exchange capabilities, direction of the use of communications and information system services, maintenance and management of the information requirement, and collation of data. Conceptual command arrangements for coalition operations are discussed more fully in chapter five.

An early task in establishing command arrangements at the operational level is the requirement for a headquarters for coalition operations in theater and a command structure. The headquarters and its staff will implement such host nation support arrangements as have been agreed; they will coordinate arrangements for civil administration in theater if this is required; they will conduct media operations in theater and foster civil-military cooperation.

---

[4] This analysis of tasks draws on the United Kingdom Draft Universal Joint Essential Task List that is the subject of ongoing work at the United Kingdom Permanent Joint Headquarters.

Alongside the command structure a liaison structure will be required to support relationships with other military and non-military agencies and institutions in theater that are outside the command structure.

The command arrangements must support the sharing of information and awareness, preparation of plans and orders, the commander's estimate, and the campaign plan and changes. They must permit the command of subordinate forces and the process of proposing Rules of Engagement (ROE's) and requesting changes to these.

The capability requirement is for operational level command, communications and planning facilities and systems. The operational level headquarters and associated communications and information systems (CIS) may need to be deployable. Depending on the particular operation, the principal elements of a headquarters could be land-based or seaborne in a suitably equipped vessel.

Generally for peacekeeping or peace enforcement operations the operational level headquarters will not need to be operationally mobile. However for certain regional conflicts the principal elements of an operational headquarters may need to relocate during the course of an operation. For example, an operation involving an amphibious insertion may first be commanded from afloat and subsequently ashore once a suitable area has been brought under control. In the longer term, the elements and functions of the operational level headquarters in theater may not necessarily in all cases be collocated. Electronic networking may permit some dispersal of elements and functions. Speed of decision is an important measure of the effectiveness of a command system. A peacekeeping operation is likely to be less demanding in this respect than a peace enforcement operation or a regional conflict.

Intelligence and Information

The planning, direction, collection and production of strategic intelligence will remain principally a national activity. However, the fusion and dissemination of strategic intelligence from national sources and its provision to the commanders of coalition operations in theater clearly has an important coalition dimension. During a NATO operation a NATO product would be available to its operational commanders.

Operational level information and intelligence tasks include planning and direction of intelligence activities, allocation of in-theater resources, collection of information, collation, correlation, evaluation, analysis and interpretation of information and its dissemination.

Capability requirements include systems for the collation, fusion, analysis and evaluation of strategic intelligence, CIS dedicated to handling intelligence material of high classification, CIS capable of providing a relevant common operational picture (RCOP) to all coalition forces and headquarters, in-theater intelligence resources including human resources, in-theater airborne, seaborne and ground based surveillance and reconnaissance assets, environmental data collection capability, and special forces with surveillance and reconnaissance capability.

In peace enforcement operations and regional conflicts there may be a requirement for ballistic missile early warning, for target acquisition information and for special forces to be able to designate targets. For peacekeeping and peace enforcement operations there may be a higher premium on intelligence drawn from human sources, but for a regional conflict the demands for military and technical intelligence will be very high.

Mobility

The tasks associated with strategic mobility into and between theaters of operation cover the planning and conduct of deployment into theater and subsequent recovery. These include examination of strategic movement options, selection and establishment of lines of communication, provision and management of strategic lift assets, execution of the movement plan including the mounting and movement of forces into theater, route clearance, and arrangements for reception, staging and onward movement. Operational mobility tasks comprise the planning and conduct of intra-theater deployment, redeployment and recovery, reception, staging and onward movement and provision of mobility and counter-mobility.

Capabilities include strategic lift in the form of aircraft and ships, and operational and tactical mobility of combat, combat support and combat service support units. Combat engineering support may be required to breach and span obstacles and otherwise to enable movement across difficult terrain. CIS capabilities will also be required to coordinate air and water space management and to prevent mutual interference between friendly units.

During regional conflict, movement is likely to be actively opposed. If strategic movement is opposed, there will be considerable demands for sea control and air superiority capabilities (see below under conduct of operations). Where operational movement is opposed, there will be a need for protection capabilities (see below) and perhaps a requirement for sea mine countermeasures as well as for the clearance of landmines and other ordnance. In addition, counter-mobility capabilities such as the ability to create land obstacles and for sea denial may be required.

Speed of movement will be a premium in regional conflicts and may be important during peace enforcement operations. Movement is likely to be more deliberate in peacekeeping operations. Movement is unlikely to be opposed during peacekeeping operations but during peace enforcement operations there may be attempts to hinder or oppose operational and tactical movement. In either case ROE's are unlikely to permit substantial counter-mobility measures.

During coalition operations mobility can be greatly enhanced if transport assets can be shared between nations and if enabling and protective capabilities can be provided by one nation to the forces of another. Adoption of common technical standards will improve the sharing of transport assets and some specific capabilities such as air to air refueling.

Conduct of Operations
Regional Conflict
The four nations' current military doctrines that would be applied in regional conflict focus on the disruption of enemy fighting capability rather than control of territory per se. Conceptual work produced by the four nations represented in this working group on the nature and patterns of future warfare indicates that this focus will continue until at least 2015. Indeed, there is likely to be greater emphasis in the longer term on attacking the cohesion of an enemy's force rather than any reversion to concepts of a linear campaign where the focus was on control and disputed control of territory. Nonetheless, control of significant areas of the battlespace is an important enabler to disruption of an enemy's fighting capability.

Tasks associated with regional conflict include the conduct of amphibious, airborne, offensive and defensive land and maritime operations, and offensive special forces operations. Ground and maritime targets must be selected for attack. Firepower resources must be allocated for this purpose. Fire support coordination measures must be implemented and the effectiveness of attacks must be evaluated. Control of significant areas of the battlespace will involve domination of key terrain, sea control operations, and offensive and active defensive counter-air operations. Specific defenses must be provided against air, ballistic missile and torpedo attack.

Command and control warfare (C^2W) will be an integral part of a response to regional conflict. Tasks will include planning and conduct of offensive and defensive operations. The elements of C^2W are electronic warfare, psychological operations, deception, operations security (OPSEC), and the physical destruction of command and control facilities.

Depending on the exact nature of the operation, the capabilities required for the conduct of operations in regional conflict might include:

- airborne and sea launched attack systems and ground based artillery;
- ground launched missile systems capable of attack on ground and maritime surface and sub-surface units;
- special forces with offensive capability;
- amphibious, airmobile and airborne ground forces;

- mechanized and light infantry, armored ground maneuver assets and mobile artillery;
- airborne maneuver assets such as attack helicopters, close air support and air interdiction capability;
- maritime sea control assets;
- offensive and defensive active and passive electronic warfare systems and other systems for offensive command and control operations;
- psychological operations capability;
- dedicated amphibious assault ships and lift assets such as air cushioned vehicles and rotary wing aircraft;
- combat search and rescue capability; and
- offensive and active defensive counter air capability, anti-missile defense, anti-torpedo defense and airspace management systems.

Synchronization of firepower and maneuver, tempo and surprise are essential to disruption of enemy warfighting capability. During coalition operations these tenets will only be achievable if there is a high degree of integration of the component capabilities of the various nations. There are therefore the highest demands for interoperability and cooperability at the operational level. In the longer term, if new concepts of network centric operations[5] are adopted by some participating nations, there will be a need for high degrees of interoperability and cooperability at the various tactical levels as well. Good interoperability and cooperability will also be essential between the forces spanning different operational environments.

Peace Enforcement
In peace enforcement operations the focus is on control of violence rather than disruption of an enemy's fighting capability. Concentration of overwhelming force to achieve simultaneity is likely to be heavily constrained by ROE's that emphasize the minimum use of force. Tasks associated with these operations include restoration of law and order, protection of humanitarian operations and human rights, containment of conflict, the forcible separation of belligerent parties, establishment and supervision of

---

[5] The concept of network centric warfare involves generating information advantage and converting it into competitive advantage. By netting a variety of users, information, and knowledge, three key capabilities would be created: shared awareness, merged planning and execution, and self-synchronized forces. These capabilities can transform the operating environment by increasing both the speed and quality of decision-making. See David S. Alberts, John J. Garstka, and Frederick P. Stein, *Network Centric Warfare: Developing and Leveraging Information Superiority* (Washington, D.C., DoD C4ISR Cooperative Research Program, 1999), 256 pp.

protected safe areas, guarantee and denial of movement, and enforcement of sanctions.

Although coalition forces will be predominantly engaged in inducement of potential and actual belligerents to acquiescence and compliance, there is a strong possibility of actual combat between coalition forces and one or more belligerent parties. Furthermore, there is the possibility that the situation may deteriorate into the outbreak of full scale combat. In these cases coalition forces may find themselves in situations similar to those of regional conflict. Military commanders and staffs will usually advise, therefore, that the capability packages fielded for peace enforcement are adequate to meet the challenge of escalation to regional conflict at least for a sufficient period to allow for the forces to be extracted.

It is not possible therefore to distinguish the capability packages required for the conduct of peace enforcement in a generic sense qualitatively from those for regional conflict. There will, however, be differences in proportions of the various capabilities, and these will reflect the risk involved in the operation and the degree of political commitment. The distinctive tasks of peace enforcement will, for instance, require adequate numbers of infantry for the various constabulary tasks. There may also be a greater emphasis on combat engineering and logistics support for humanitarian operations and for restoration of local infrastructure.

Peacekeeping
Conventional peacekeeping tasks consist of observing and monitoring events as well as the disposition and posture of former combatants, supervision of truces and cease-fires, interposition along cease-fire lines and in demilitarized areas, provision of transition assistance, demobilization, cantonment and disarmament, provision of humanitarian relief and its protection, and provision of explosive ordnance (mine) clearance.

In complex emergencies it is unlikely that peacekeeping tasks will be so clear cut. There may, for instance, be uncertainties as to the degree and permanence of consent among the former belligerents. There may also be a temporary or permanent collapse of local government and infrastructure, and a need therefore for emphasis on humanitarian relief, temporary military government, and the provision of law and order.

Conduct of peacekeeping operations requires adequate infantry for constabulary duties, and combat engineering and logistics support for humanitarian operations as well as for restoration of local infrastructure. In a deteriorating situation peacekeeping forces would customarily be evacuated. The option may, however, be taken to reinforce them with the additional capabilities required for peace enforcement.

Representative Mission Challenges

During peacekeeping operations the need to disrupt enemy combat capability would not normally apply except at a low tactical level in the case of a minor skirmish. The use of military force is usually measured and deliberate and there is not normally a requirement for the degrees of simultaneity, tempo and surprise demanded by the other missions.

Force Protection
Force protection tasks include provision of physical protection to one's own forces, to logistics support and other constituencies, conduct of counter-surveillance, countering the effects of enemy conventional attack by passive defense, recuperation from the effects of enemy conventional attack, protection against battlespace hazards, and establishment of disaster control measures. These tasks entail provision of personnel security and information security, defense of key points and lines of support, and integration where relevant with host nation security arrangements.

Depending on the nature of the threat, NBC protection and defense against theater ballistic and cruise missile attack may also be required. Individual units at every level of echelonment will usually be equipped to provide a certain degree of individual protection. Beyond this level of protection capabilities will be contributed by other units. In the coalition context these capabilities may come from the forces of other nations and there may therefore be a dependency of the forces of one nation on those of others for survival. Such dependency requires a high level of technical and doctrinal interoperability and cooperability and implies a considerable degree of trust. These demands for interoperability will clearly be highest in a regional conflict. However national sensitivities to modest levels of casualties in elective operations result in an emphasis on force protection in all operations. In peace enforcement operations in particular, this protection might be extended to large numbers of civilian personnel and infrastructure.

Specific NBC protection capabilities include provision of detection, identification and monitoring, warning and reporting, individual and collective protection, hazard management and medical countermeasures and support. Capabilities to protect against ballistic and cruise missile attack include early warning (see information and intelligence above), detection, and engagement of missiles.

While the NBC and conventional ballistic and cruise missile threat might today be associated principally with regional conflict, in the longer term these may become weapons of asymmetric response that could be deployed by disgruntled groups during more benign operations. For this reason, NBC and theater missile protection may even be a factor during a peacekeeping operation following a complex emergency. The sophisticated capabilities that these forms of protection require are unlikely to be available to all coalition partners. Protection may therefore place demands of interoperability, cooperability and trust on coalition partners in all of the three missions.

Sustainment

Force sustainment tasks include supply of provisions, water, spare parts, fuel and lubricants, maintenance and repair of equipment, provision of transportation, provision of personnel and personal support services, medical services and health support and legal services. The military will have to select and establish forward maintenance bases (FMB's) and fuel depots as well as a rear support area, and to provide for refugees and prisoners of war.

In a regional conflict there are likely to be considerably higher levels of consumption of ammunition, of demands on repair organizations, and of casualties requiring medical treatment than for the other missions. Furthermore, in a regional conflict logistics may be a vulnerability of a coalition that an enemy will try to target either conventionally or through asymmetric attacks. There will therefore be a need to minimize the logistics footprint in theater to maximize protection. The footprint can be reduced by speed of delivery and by efficient use of logistics resources. A high degree of logistics interoperability among coalition partners will improve efficient use.

The problems of achieving logistics interoperability depend on the nature of the service. These problems are exacerbated when a coalition includes partners who are not NATO members. There are cultural differences in accepting food products of certain types and standards of quality. There are also cultural differences in medical practices. There are variations in quality of medical service and therefore in the confidence that national authorities will have in the ability of the medical services of other nations to care for their personnel adequately.

NATO has achieved some successful standardization of ammunition, fuel and lubricants, but the highest levels of standardization are not achievable without close coordination of equipment acquisition. Similarly, interoperability in spare parts and maintenance is largely a matter of commonality of equipment, although the use of commercial-off-the-shelf technology in some categories of equipment may allow for a greater exchange of spare parts in the future. Maintenance may be provided as a common service for simpler tasks only.

Forces structured, equipped and provisioned for traditional styles of warfighting place demands on transportation assets that can be extremely difficult to meet. Additional overheads are typically imposed if those forces are multinational. This adds weight to coalition efforts to improve the ability to deploy coherent, effective forces.

Nations may give priority to their own forces in the use of national transport assets. There are likely to be some technical problems in the common use of transport assets, particularly when large vehicles and equipment or dangerous cargoes are to be moved, but these will be minor in comparison to that of the willingness to provide scarce national assets for common purposes.

Differences in Capability Requirements across the Three Missions
Table I on the following two pages summarizes the principal differences in capabilities demanded by the three representative missions.

MAINTAINING COALITION POLITICAL AND MILITARY COHESION

Countries that form a coalition to intervene in a given crisis or conflict can only do so on the basis of some level of shared interest and objectives. The four countries involved in this study share a large core of strategic interests and values. Nonetheless, the national interests of all coalition participants in a specific crisis or conflict will rarely be identical due to geopolitical, historical, cultural, and domestic political factors.

Thus, national agendas and perceptions will complicate agreement on a mission's political objectives. The inherent nature of regional conflicts may force resolution on these political objectives quickly; however, the same is not necessarily the case for peacekeeping and peace enforcement operations. Yet, as discussed above, speed of decision-making may be politically and militarily essential in a peace enforcement operation, and politically important in a peacekeeping operation. Decision-makers may tend to operate on a false timeline given misperceptions of the magnitude of the contingency.

Adversaries may tend to take advantage of the time lapse and in some cases may deliberately maintain a lower level to the crisis to avoid drawing too much attention or concern. Part of their efforts will no doubt include information operations, again clouding the picture. Adding further complexity, they may focus these operations against critical members of the coalition or supporting states that are be in a position to provide access or transit of forces to the theater of operations.

Even when most coalition members strongly support the central political objectives of an intervention, as was the case with *Operation Allied Force* in Kosovo, national agendas and perceptions can lead to divergent views over the best means of achieving those objectives. This phenomenon was manifest in the Kosovo operation, where allies disagreed over critical issues such as the use of ground forces and what targets to strike in the air campaign. Clearly, the greater the extent to which coalition members can harmonize their political and military objectives for an intervention, the easier it will be

Table 1 (part one): Differences in Capability Requirements across the Three Missions

	Regional conflict	Peace enforcement	Peacekeeping
Command arrangements	a. Operational level headquarters strategically and operationally mobile. b. Speed of decision-making militarily essential.	a. Operational level headquarters strategically mobile. b. Speed of decision-making politically and militarily important and potentially essential.	a. Operational level headquarters strategically mobile. b. Speed of decision-making politically important
Information and intelligence	a. Early warning. b. Target acquisition information c. Special forces to designate targets. d. Premium on military and technical intelligence.	a. Possible need for: early warning of long-range missile attack; target acquisition information; special forces to designate targets. b. Premium on human source intelligence.	a. Premium on human source intelligence.
Mobility	a. Counter-mobility measures. b. Protection and control of environment essential for operational and tactical mobility - possibly for strategic mobility. c. Premium on speed of movement.	a. Counter-mobility measures restrained. b. Protection for operational and tactical mobility may be necessary. c. Speed of movement may be important	a. Counter-mobility measures not normally permitted. b. Movement may be more deliberate.

Table 1 (part two): Differences in Capability Requirements across the Three Missions

	Regional Conflict	Peace Enforcement	Peacekeeping
Conduct of Operations	a. Full range of ground, sea and air delivered offensive and defensive combat capabilities to deliver maneuver and firepower depending on nature of operation. b. Systems for offensive command and control operations. c. Combat search and rescue capability. d. Combat air space management systems. e. High degree of integration of component capabilities of fighting formations.	a. Quantitative rather than qualitative distinctions in capabilities from those required for regional conflict. b. Adequate numbers of infantry for constabulary tasks. c. Combat engineering and logistics support for humanitarian operations and for restoration of local infrastructure.	a. Adequate infantry for constabulary duties. b. Combat engineering and logistics support for humanitarian operations and for restoration of local infrastructure. c. Use of military force is usually measured and deliberate. Not normally a requirement for the degrees of simultaneity, tempo and surprise.
Force Protection	a. High levels of protection necessary for own forces and those of coalition partners, placing big demands on trust, cooperability and interoperability. b. Protection against long-range missile threat and NBC attack a likely requirement.	a. Political aversion to casualties demands that protection of own forces will be a dominant consideration for some partners. b. It is likely to be necessary and a mission objective to offer protection to non-combatants. c. Risk of asymmetric response means that protection against long-range missile and CBW attack may be a requirement in the longer term.	a. It may be necessary at the tactical level to offer occasional protection to some non-combatants. b. Risk of asymmetric response as a herald to a deteriorating situation means that protection against long-range missile and CBW attack may be a consideration for the longer term.
Sustainment	a. High levels of consumption of ammunition, of demands for repair, and of casualties. b. Need to protect logistics from concerted attack and minimize logistics footprint by speed of delivery and efficient use of resources.	a. Lower levels of consumption of ammunition, demands for repair and of casualties. b. Need to protect logistics from occasional concerted attack	a. Modest levels of consumption of ammunition and of casualties. b. Need to protect logistics from criminal activity.

to maintain the coalition's cohesion while minimizing reductions in military effectiveness.[6]

Ethnic conflict in Europe has arguably not threatened U.S. national interests to the same extent as it has those of many European NATO members. U.S. participation in European peace support and crisis management operations has consequently taken place on a more fragile political basis than has been the case for the major European contributors to these operations. Political controversy in Washington over whether sufficient national interests are at stake in European peace support and crisis management interventions to warrant direct U.S. military participation has in turn led to a strong emphasis on robust force protection in U.S. planning and conduct of these operations. European countries must be prepared in the future to carry out these operations without direct U.S. participation if Washington feels that U.S. national interests are not sufficiently engaged, as well as ensure that they have the ability to make a balanced and significant military contribution in cases where U.S. armed forces do participate directly. As discussed in the preceding chapter, these are indeed two of the major goals of the European Union's new security and defense policy.

During operational planning, the rule of law will constrain the actions of intervening coalitions. This is not necessarily the case for local adversarial forces that do not abide by the same value system. Adversaries will exploit coalition seams early on to deter or influence the force generation process. ROE's will face a similar challenge, particularly within peacekeeping missions. Divergent interpretation of ROE's within the coalition will complicate the operational picture and expose vulnerable seams within the coalition itself. This will allow for ready exploitation by potential adversaries.

Command and control of the overall coalition operation will always be politically sensitive for the various partners. The transfer of authority to a joint and combined task force commander is necessary to ensure the unity of effort. However, coalition partners will normally transfer this authority only if they are confident that the commander will follow agreed policy and doctrine.

Regardless of the acceptance level of casualties, the issue of force protection becomes crucial at the onset of deployment operations. Assessing the nature and level of the threat is critical to the safety and effectiveness of coalition forces. Due to the selective perceptions of adversarial forces, some members of the coalition could be at greater risk of attack. Historical animosities and cultural bias easily jade the notions and motives both for the adversary and coalition partners. The latter may inadvertently place

---

[6] For additional discussion on decision-making within a coalition, read Edouard Valensi, "On Decision-Making in Coalition", Appendix A.

themselves at greater risk due to the actions and misperceptions of local players in the theater of operations.

Actual or threatened attacks against the national territory as well as the deployed forces of coalition members will constitute a prime means for local adversaries to attempt to split intervening coalitions apart. As noted in the discussion in the previous chapter, adversaries could undertake homeland attacks via both terrorism and long-range delivery systems, including with NBC weapons. Non-military participants in peace support operations will also become the target of forces opposed to the intervention. If non-military participants are forced to depart, the intervening coalition will not be able to carry out civil reconstruction activities and will be unable to achieve a political end state that would allow for the withdrawal of military forces.

The acquisition of capabilities to provide for both homeland defense and force protection is largely a national responsibility. However, greater intelligence exchange and collaborative threat assessment can play an essential role in helping to thwart attacks on national territory and deployed forces, as well as greatly facilitate the elaboration of shared political and military objectives among coalition partners. Exchanges of intelligence have always been easier and more complete at the battlefield than at the strategic level, but the two levels are merging. What used to be strategic intelligence is increasingly relevant to what happens on the battlefield, as well as to more broadly enabling the coalition to deal with the kinds of threats that can greatly strain its cohesion.

Decisive coalition action will depend on allies reaching quick consensus on threat perceptions. The fact that future security challenges will spring from a growing diversity of national and transnational sources will make them ever more unpredictable and difficult to characterize. While battlespace is dominated by operational military considerations, crisis space is far more heterogeneous and complex, involving the full economic, political, religious, and ecological dimensions of the international security environment.[7] Crises that precede or accompany force projection operations are all composed of some combination of these elements.

The risks and challenges to intelligence fall into two broad categories; integration within the coalition and the nature of the operational environment. In both of these, technology and human resources will be a constant source of challenge. The collection of human intelligence and the rapid dissemination between coalition partners has been and will be as critical as technical capabilities in addressing peace operations and regional conflict. This is particularly true in trying adequately to anticipate or understand the

---

[7] Dennis M. Gormley and Douglas M. Hart, "Extending Network-Centric Warfare to Coalition Crisis Management and Assessment", Appendix B.

true intent of the adversaries in the more non-permissive environments. Information operations will become an increasing threat to intelligence operations and infrastructure out to 2015, particularly at the coalition seams. Adversaries could attempt to "cloud" the common operational picture through the introduction of inaccurate or voluminous information. In the absence of a collaborative intelligence effort within the coalition, perceptions could easily vary due to a host of factors, including socio-cultural biases.

NATO's member nations possess impressive resources that could be employed to map, navigate, and exploit crisis space to safeguard their collective economies and societies, but these assets are currently misdirected and used piecemeal on traditional diplomatic or military venues. A broader approach is now required compared with NATO's traditional, heavy focus on military intelligence. NATO countries must possess the ability rapidly to form analytical communities of interest that can thoroughly aggregate threat related assessments in order to anticipate and keep pace with emerging crises while safeguarding unique intelligence sources and methods from compromise.

FINDINGS

Because the information dimensions of crisis space are so daunting, and the data collection capabilities of NATO member countries potentially so extensive, maximum use must be made of information technology in order to derive warning, plan collaboratively, and act collectively as early in a crisis as possible.

- Realistic blue/red wargaming could prove extremely valuable in obtaining better insight regarding adversary concepts of the use of asymmetric threats. Much can be done to improve understanding of adversary thinking that does not involve exchanges of classified information. Sufficient insight into adversary concepts will not come through traditional fused intelligence. Blue/red wargaming is likely to prove more fruitful.

DEVELOPMENT OBJECTIVES

The working group proposes the creation of a four country threat analysis program, to include the establishment of data bases for the related contingencies. This program would operate in confidentiality utilizing open sources and unclassified information. The program's output could be selectively available for publication. The program would organize the following types of activities:

- Develop a common methodology to assess the impact of threats and conduct analysis of alternative futures in the security environment as well as their implications.

- Assess the incorporation of extant and emerging technologies in asymmetric approaches to warfare.

- Undertake analysis of adversary intentions, including the use of asymmetric threats. This analysis would derive in part from a red team "psyops" study of how future adversaries will act. It would serve both as an introduction to red/blue wargaming (see below) and as an independent analysis of adversary will and intent.

- Conduct realistic red/blue, n-sided war-gaming to analyze current threats and identify emerging ones.

- Evaluate new information technology tools for improved NATO crisis management, and make recommendations to governments regarding the use of these tools.

- Undertake a vulnerability assessment of current and potential coalitions. This assessment would work in tandem with the Red Team psyops analysis. It is important to know not only how the adversary thinks and plans, but also what it may see in coalition participants that may not be readily apparent to the participants themselves, where it can exploit vulnerabilities, and how the coalition members can fix or hide those vulnerabilities.

- Highlight hot spots that may call for coalition operations in the future. This effort would be a by-product of the preceding threat analysis recommendations. It would not be designed to supplant various national or NATO strategic warning efforts, but rather complement them or provide a start for further research and analysis.

III. NATURE OF INTEROPERABILITY: CHALLENGES FOR THE FUTURE

NEW DIMENSIONS OF INTEROPERABILITY AND COOPERABILITY

Technical interoperability is neither essential nor sufficient to achieve desirable coalition behaviors. It is not sufficient because an exchange of data with an inadequate ability to understand and act on this data does not advance the cause. It is not essential because organization, doctrine and procedures have an impact on coalition operations. They can be designed to make up for a lack of complete or perfect technical interoperability. However, to achieve the level of effectiveness that the working group seeks for coalition operations, emphasizing cohesion and responsiveness, coalition partners need to be interoperable at three levels: technical, cognitive, and organizational and doctrinal (see Figure 2).

Figure 2: Levels of Interoperability

	Level	Product	Example Measures
Co-operability	Organizational /Doctrinal (Work Exchange)	Synchronization (Unity of Effort)	Force Efficiency: • Target Engagement • Resource Consumption
Interoperability	Cognitive (Knowledge Exchange)	Shared Understanding	Common Perception of Adversary: • Capabilities • Intentions
	Technical (Data Exchange)	Common Relevant Operational Picture	CROP: • Completeness • Currency

To achieve a significant degree of interoperability, coalitions need not only to realize technical interoperability, but also to achieve "cooperability". The working group coined the term "cooperability" to mean successfully bridging different differences in doctrine, organization and culture. Achieving cooperability allows different coalition partners not only to exchange data, but to understand its implications and to synchronize operations.

NATO's formal definition of interoperability is, "the ability of systems, units, or forces to provide services to and accept services from other systems, units, and forces and to use these services so exchanged to enable them to operate effectively together"[8]. Like most existing NATO definitions, this one was developed in the context of war fighting and a formal alliance structure.

---

[8] NATO Standardization Agreement, AAP-6.

However, as the world has changed, the need for interoperability has also changed in several ways. For example, NATO has recently adopted the term "operational interoperability", which is similar to the idea of cooperability used by this working group. It recognizes that interoperability is not limited to the narrow technical dimension of simply tying systems together to exchange data, but involves as well the ability of coalition partners to share information, create a shared understanding of the situation, collaborate on the development and selection of courses of action, communicate these to all forces or units, and allow forces to work together effectively.

MAJOR CHALLENGES

Change of Environment

Four major changes in the security environment result in the need to reexamine traditional ways of viewing interoperability. First, the very idea of "effectiveness" forces the concept of interoperability beyond its traditional military framework. When military victory constitutes the goal of a mission, the primary concern is how to achieve force effectiveness. However, when the mission objective is significantly political and humanitarian, as it has been in cases like Somalia, Cambodia, Bosnia, and Kosovo, the purpose of coalition military operations becomes to support policy effectiveness. In such circumstances, it is distinctly possible to achieve the military mission in ways that undermine the political goals of the coalition.

Second, as the study members have recognized in selecting the missions to be analyzed, the missions undertaken by coalitions have changed from war fighting to primarily peace operations, national support operations, and humanitarian assistance. These missions include significant political, social, and economic components. The military may be the source of essential services such as creating a secure environment, setting up effective communications, and providing transportation. Nonetheless, these services are not sufficient to accomplish the mission. Even more important, these services are often provided to non-military entities such as international organizations (IO), non-governmental organizations (NGO), private voluntary organizations (PVO), and host nation support. Even within the coalition member countries, services are often provided by non-military agencies with relief and reconstruction missions. Hence, for coalition effectiveness in these mission types, interoperability may extend well beyond the military arena.

Third, while implied in the NATO definition, the extent to which information is a crucial element in interoperability today is not stressed adequately. As a way of coordinating and focusing their activities to ensure that they are effective, coalition military forces and the variety of actors with which they work today rely heavily on exchanging:

- data;
- information, or data that has been organized and is presented in context;
- knowledge, or data that includes cause and effect as well as vision into the future; and
- understanding, meaning the common perception of coalition tasks and the principles of how to operate.

Moreover, because coalition forces are often operating in a competitive, multi-sided situation, the security of the information being exchanged and supplied is also important.

Fourth, the member nations have become involved in more and more coalitions with partners who are not formally allies. Formal allies, like NATO countries, have long-term commitments and opportunities to both acquire compatible systems and to work together in exercises to develop greater interoperability. Coalitions often include members whose military forces have neither compatible equipment nor prior opportunities to work together.

Technology as a Discriminatory Factor

The study group noted that the pace of change in information technology also threatens interoperability. If one or a small number of nations develops technical military capabilities that are not matched by others and are incompatible with the systems and capabilities of others, then creating and maintaining interoperability at the "state of the art" level become almost impossible. This disconnect can occur because of unwillingness to share advanced technology, because not all coalition members can afford the most advanced systems, or because the nations choose incompatible technical approaches. The alternative, choosing to work at the level of "lowest common denominator" technologies, would handicap the best coalition forces and needlessly reduce mission effectiveness.

Interoperability Payoffs Seen as Uncertain

While widely acknowledged as important, interoperability and cooperability require investments of time, money, and intellectual capital. Improvements in interoperability and cooperability can only be established through a shared vision, coordinated acquisition programs, cooperative training and exercises, and willingness to consider allied and coalition partner perspectives. The necessary investments have often proven difficult to justify because most defense establishments consider cooperability and interoperability to be intangibles, like morale. Because they are considered intangibles, their payoffs are seen as uncertain. Hence priority often goes to weapons platforms and additional force structure, which are perceived to have more readily calculable and tangible payoffs. However, having failed to make these investments, coalitions are often condemned to repeatedly experience interoperability and cooperability problems. Hence, many of the "lessons learned" (perhaps best termed lessons recorded) deal with coalition interoperability and cooperability shortfalls from a variety of operations such as Somalia, Bosnia, and Kosovo.

How to Tackle these New Challenges?

Technical interoperability and cooperability are inseparable; they are both essential if coalition operations are to be effective. The true goal consists of assembling effective coalition "Mission Capability Packages (MCP's)". MCP's are composed of information, communications and weapons systems that are technically compatible, and that are employed by harmonized command structures based on compatible organizations and doctrines, which together support mutually agreed concepts of coalition operations (see Figure 3).

Figure 3: Mission Capability Packages

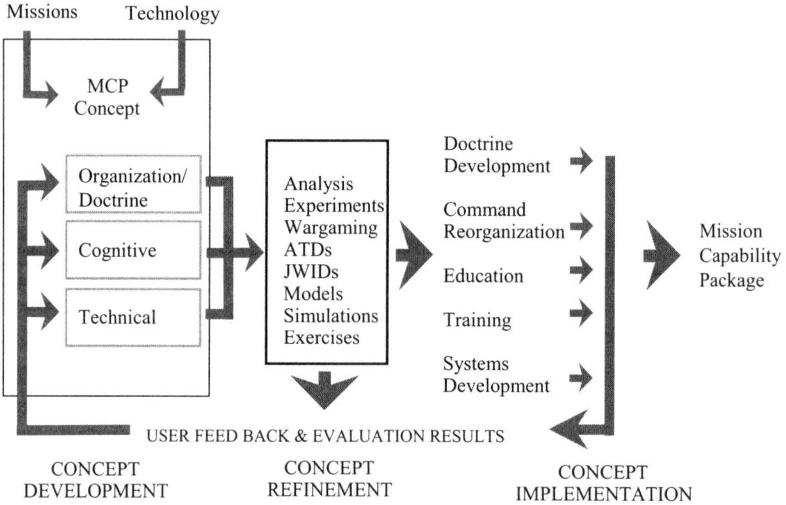

Adapted from C4ISR Cooperative Research Program (CCRP) Initiatives Briefing

The working group focused considerable attention on the command, control, communications, computers, intelligence, surveillance, and reconnaissance (C^4ISR) aspects of a coalition MCP. While physical interoperability, such as forces that use the same caliber of ammunition or aircraft that use the same types of fuel, is valuable and important, C^4ISR is crucial for at least three reasons. First, physical incompatibility can be overcome with proper C^4ISR; for example, forces with different logistics needs can be supported from different locations. Second, the keys to cooperability are in the C^4ISR arena: pooled sensor data, common operational picture, synchronized planning and execution. Third, the information, knowledge, and communications technologies that enable C⁴ISR are advancing rapidly. As a result, there are differences in the rate that coalition partners are adopting new technology as well as in the manner that they are adapting their concepts of operation, organizations and doctrine to leverage the new capabilities being provided. Hence a major thrust of this study focuses on C⁴ISR interoperability and the resulting mission capability packages for the missions of interest.

ASSESSING THE VALUE OF INTEROPERABILITY IN COALITION OPERATIONS

Despite the "prevailing wisdom" that interoperability and cooperability are intangibles and cannot easily be measured or their impact on mission effectiveness ascertained, they are, in fact, excellent candidates for empirical analyses and for coordinated experimentation among allies and potential coalition partners. For example, five different levels of technical interoperability have been posited:

- no interoperability - incompatible systems and services;
- "swivel chair interoperability" - the output or services from one system can be used by another, but only when a user takes the results from one system and converts it for use in the other;
- partial interoperability - some parts of the output (for example, message categories and addresses) can be transferred directly, but other parts must be transformed for use;
- confederation - different systems or services are linked in ways that do not interfere with the operation of either, but each is able to service the other (this implies the use of an automatic transformation); and
- integration - systems and services are performed in one fully coupled system.

The general metrics by which cooperability can be measured are also relatively well understood. They include a number of factors recognized in NATO's Code of Best Practice for C^2 Analyses:

- measures of qualities inherent in the system;
- measures of systems performance;
- measures of C^2 effectiveness;
- measures of force effectiveness; and
- measures of policy effectiveness.

Moreover, they also include a system of observable measures or metrics that address the performance of key parts of the C^2 cycle:

- measures of the ability to monitor the operational environment - the quality of information available in terms of its completeness, currency, accuracy, precision, and consistency;
- measures of the quality of shared understandings of the situation and how they can evolve;
- measures of the quality of the process by which alternative courses of action are created;
- measures of the quality of the process by which alternative courses of action are assessed;
- measures of the quality of the process by which decisions are made;
- measures of the quality of the directives and requests for support that are created and disseminated by the C^2 system;
- measures of the ability of the C^2 system to create queries for information and respond to such queries; and
- measures of the quality of reports created in the C^2 system.

Cross-cutting metrics such as the speed of the military decision-making process, the percentage of time that elements of the force are operating without guidance or plans from superiors because the pace of change in the situation is faster than the C^2 system, and the improved likelihood of mission accomplishment, are also relevant. At this point, the approach to command and control, including the level of autonomy left to the different elements of the force, should be considered as a key factor as it directly relates to the degree of efficiency in any interoperable architecture.

Moreover, the hypotheses applicable to these analyses are also well understood. For example, recent writing on network centric warfare argues that military organizations with better linkages can expect the following payoffs:

- improved awareness of the operating environment, because they can consider information from more sources, earlier;
- improved shared awareness, because they will see a more common picture; and
- improved synchronization, because of greater coordination over time and space as well as greater understanding of the opportunities and threats relevant to all elements in the coalition.

Moreover advocates of the network centric approach also argue that it should make decisions faster, not just better. As an optimum, it is recognized that receiving the relevant information on time and being able to exploit it at each level constitutes the basis for the efficiency of the force. Thus, coupling the relevance of information with its timely transmission makes a good starting point for building evolutionary cooperability procedures.

NATO EFFORTS AND ACTIVITIES TO ENHANCE ALLIED INTEROPERABILITY

Systematic efforts by NATO to improve interoperability in adjusting to new challenges originated mainly from its C^3I (command, control, communications and intelligence) communities a few years ago. They began to lobby successfully for elevating "interoperability", which until then had denoted a specific category and level of "technical" standardization, to a higher and richer conceptual level. In the meantime, the quest for interoperability has assumed a high profile in operational and even political terms. This is reflected in NATO's new Strategic Concept, in particular in its "Guidelines for Defense" section, as well as in other documents of the 1999 Washington Summit. Most directly, the adoption and promotion of NATO's DCI are focused on improving future interoperability across the board. To that effect NATO nations and military authorities have agreed on key areas for improvement and enabling factors, which were, however, broken down into a long list of diverse action items that remain to be structured in terms of priorities. In addition they have created procedures and adapted machinery in order to facilitate and speed up coordination among and within NATO's complex network of committees and agencies as well as in capitals.

It is too early to assess how far this extraordinary effort will succeed. But there is no doubt that the comprehensive and interactive approach chosen is designed and has potential to generate significant political and bureaucratic leverage for addressing and dealing with key shortcomings, challenges and forward looking concepts. In the ongoing review and adaptation of NATO's overall strategy, operational doctrine, command structure, and force structure, political and military leaders have singled out the enhancement of interoperability as a priority issue. In this context, the political and operational requirements for non-Article V force projection and coalition operations are receiving special attention.

Clearly, such innovative approaches reflect the problems incurred and insights gained by NATO governments and authorities during operations in Bosnia and Kosovo. In this vein NATO is pursuing a comprehensive approach cutting across established domains and perspectives. And its major commanders favor complementing current pragmatic adaptive measures by the exploration of more radical innovative options. It is also addressing the possibility of including partners into these efforts as far as possible.

In terms of organizing concepts, force goals, and capability packages, the modernization and strengthening of NATO's multinational formations stand out. Special emphasis is being given to the future organization of headquarters and their CIS capacities.

The CJTF concept is being exercised and tested. CJTF's are defined as task forces organized and formed for contingency operations that require multi-national and multi-service command and control. They are required to be deployable, survivable, and sustainable, and to be suitable for Article V and non-Article V contingencies, particularly for crisis management and peace support operations. One maritime and two land-based CJTF headquarters are planned. Their C^2 capabilities are expected to include communications from the strategic to the tactical level, creation of a common operational picture, the ability to integrate NATO and non-NATO augmentees, and the standard NATO staff functions. This general agreement on CJTF's can be expected to become a "forcing function" that drives NATO thinking and planning from the ream of the theoretical toward the more practical issues involved in organizing and managing forces.

Supreme Headquarters Allied Powers Europe (SHAPE) has developed a concept for upgrading and modernizing NATO's Allied Mobile Force, Land (AMF[L]) to a multinational reaction force of up to division size. It is designed as a suitable lead force for any operation, for example as a crisis management tool for Article V planning situations as well as an initial entry and enabling force for non-Article V missions. It will implement innovative structures for echeloned force build up and a common force pool providing a capability to adapt rapidly to changing requirements. AMF[L]'s integrated headquarters will have a modular structure and its C^3 system will fully exploit the innovative potential state-of-the-art information technology. It is notable that this CIS concept will be assessed and tested in the first NATO sponsored trial by means of the Concept Development and Joint & Combined Experimentation program under the lead of Allied Command Atlantic (ACLANT).

NATO's C^3 Vision and Interoperability Strategy

NATO is developing its C^3 Interoperability Management Plan (NIMP), an important element of the NATO Interoperability Framework (NIF). The NIMP describes the strategy and implementation policy for C^3 interoperability and includes details about the interoperability products (plans, standards, and documentation) applicable to NATO or to nationally owned C^3 systems used by NATO forces. NATO is also in the process of developing a set of Allied Joint Doctrines that describe the organization and the principles of allied operations. Once ratified by the majority of the NATO nations they will become official NATO documents and constitute Standardization Agreements (STANAG).

NATO's C^3 vision foresees a NATO-wide integrated system of systems able to present the appropriate information at relevant levels, incorporate mission planning and decision-making tools, and support decentralized execution of operations. Further, the NATO C^3 system together with national systems are expected to be capable of supporting the complete spectrum of operations for all C^3 levels and associated mission areas. The

NATO C^3 System will have both secure and clear voice, facsimile, data, and video communications capabilities, as well as access to a wide variety of communications media, including wire, fiber optics, and high frequency satellite. Common NATO wide area networks will link these sites. Users will be able to access distant data bases and share common information, including intelligence. The vision foresees only one information system on which all services will be provided. The vision emphasizes services, not specific systems, in order to encourage the search for common solutions. NATO is seeking a common approach in program management, integration of commercial products, security management, and data management in order to achieve effective sharing of information between systems, including data exchange, remote services, electronic mail, video conferencing, collaborative software, and information broadcast. The NIMP identifies several factors that affect the strategy:

- Legacy Systems: Interoperability within NATO is currently based largely on the exchange of formatted, character oriented messages and the use of tactical data links. These capabilities do not allow for the range of services envisioned. As a consequence, in spite of the existence of operationally validated interoperability requirements, many C^2 systems installed and used throughout NATO cannot directly share data. Emerging C^3 system architectures and plans must account for such legacy systems without being constrained by them.
- Heterogeneity: Despite NATO efforts to increase the degree of commonality and homogeneity, the overall C^3 system environment will remain a complex mixture of common and partially common funded and nationally acquired systems. Hence, planning, cooperation, and some degree of standardization are essential to provide operational interoperability.
- Flexibility and Adaptability: The unpredictability of future operations requires C^3 systems that are flexible and can adapt their performance and functionality broadly. Moreover, to avoid early obsolescence in an era of rapidly changing technologies, C^3 systems must be able to accommodate new standards and technologies.
- Security, Integrity, Availability and Assurance: Operational interoperability and shared information access bring with them risks to security.
- Testing Technical Assurance, Validation, and Conformance: The NATO C^3 Interoperability Testing Infrastructure (NIETI) is an essential supporting element of the NATO C^3 Interoperability Environment (NIE). NATO envisions a rigorous process of verification, validation, and testing as systems are designed and implemented.

Implementing the Vision

The establishment and implementation of an overall C^3 system architecture is perceived as one important step by NATO. The goal is to agree on the architecture for the core system within the next three years. Three views of the architecture are needed:

- the operational view, which consists of information needs, their exchange patterns between organizations and in functional terms, and locations of the nodes;
- the systems view, comprising the mapping of information flows and hardware; and
- a technical view.

The Rolling Interoperability Plan (RIP) is seen as a key document that will help establish short and long term goals, specify milestones, interoperability requirements, and interoperability shortfalls. This document will cover a 5-6 year time span and will provide visibility and oversight for progress toward the vision.

In order to promote interoperability and as a first step toward realizing the vision, the Major NATO Commanders (MNC) have been working together on the Allied Command Europe (ACE) Allied Command and Control Information System (ACCIS) Implementation Plan, and on the capability packages to establish core headquarters facilities. With the support of the NATO C^3 Agency (NC^3A), they are now developing the Bi-MNC Target Architectural Framework. This project means that NATO will soon have a single foundation, or core capability, on which to build specific applications. Connecting the Supreme Allied Commander, Europe (SACEUR) and the Supreme Allied Commander, Atlantic (SACLANT) using a single core capability is a required first step toward the NATO C^3 "system of the future". Several principles have been agreed upon, including the adoption of a common ACCIS core system, open systems to the maximum extent possible, modular software designs, and the maximum use of industry standards and commercial products.

The concepts of the SHAPE Immediate Response Task Force, Land (IRTF-L) and of the CJTF's to be developed represent other important implementation arenas. As these initiatives are converted from ideas into real organizations with forces at their disposal, whether in real world situations or exercises, they will provide realistic feedback on the viability of NATO's vision in the C^4ISR interoperability arena. NATO's C^3 Board has been nominated as the lead body for nine DCI action items and as a supporting organization for a further eight, all of which are more or less focusing on improving interoperability between alliance forces.

Nature of Interoperability: Challenges for the Future

In parallel to these activities, NATO is creating a new hierarchy of Allied Joint Publications. Their role is to create a common understanding on principles and procedures to enhance interoperability and cooperability. Nations will discuss their different points of view and create common doctrine. The five-year AJP development plan includes doctrine for CJTF operations.

INTEROPERABILITY SUCCESSES AND ISSUES

Clearly one of the important successes in this arena is the widespread recognition that interoperability is an important issue that is affecting coalition performance. With that recognition, efforts are being undertaken to improve the situation, the NATO efforts cited above being a very good example. Other efforts, some of them bilateral and others involving several countries are also underway. For example, Joint Warfare Interoperability Demonstrations (JWID's) have resulted in the creation of a Combined Wide Area Network (CWAN) involving NATO and Australia. Plans exist to use this CWAN as the basis for a Combined Federated Battle Laboratory (CFBL) intended to examine technical interoperability problems.

The October 1999 Multi-National Working Group exercises with Australia, Canada, France, Germany, the UK and the US again have shown how hard and time consuming putting together a coalition can be. This exercise among nations that practice together all the time shows how little coalition partners are able to learn from the past when it comes to implementing actions in cooperability. Participants expect other nations to join the activity. Moreover, both NATO and the four nations represented in this working group have undertaken a variety of lessons learned (or at least recorded) analyses that have highlighted the need for more and better cooperability and interoperability.

However, awareness is not the only requirement for progress. First, the formal issues that have emerged are almost totally in the arenas of technical interoperability, with much less emphasis on the more difficult arena of cooperability. As the working group has noted, the relatively isolated arena of technical interoperability is only the visible tip of a much larger iceberg that includes the need for all the elements of mission capability packages: compatible doctrines, concepts of operation, procedures, training, and organizations. The working group noted that for these elements a solution to interoperability problems requires direction and guidance at the strategic level. The issues go far beyond military responsibility.

Moreover, key policy areas, particularly technological leadership, information sharing and information assurance, are not being addressed in appropriate ways. Even within the four nations represented in this study, issues have arisen about ensuring the integrity of national technological capabilities and the need to find ways to confederate disparate systems purchased nationally. Similarly, the four nations all recognize the legitimate need to preserve some nationally obtained information, in particular intelligence, but also recognize the need for broad sharing of data, information, and knowledge. How the tension between these two legitimate perspectives will be resolved has a major impact on the level of interoperability and cooperability that can be achieved. Finally, information sharing creates threats to information assurance. Each nation, and each coalition, must also resolve this fundamental tension.

The vast majority of current efforts deal with military to military interoperability and cooperability. However, most of the missions likely to be undertaken by coalitions involve other actors, including non-military government agencies, NGO's, PVO's, IO's, and host governments. These non-military actors have important roles to play; often possess key data, information, and knowledge important for mission success; and need to be linked into common situation understandings, planning, and execution.

Some of these non-military partners, and the military establishments of some states likely to be involved in future coalitions are also "technologically disadvantaged" when compared with the most modern militaries:

- Variations in national C^4 cycles and practices will be problematic if not addressed prior to deployment. In addition, technological differences will become evident between coalition partners throughout the course of the entire operation. Common systems and platforms do not necessarily have to be the final solution so long as interfaces or integration can be achieved.
- Some coalition partners with prolonged resource constraints may not have now or ever the advanced technological capabilities and skill of other members. Most of the formal interoperability efforts underway focus on future systems and high-end technologies, with limited focus on the crucial issues of linkages and compatibility with less capable partners. Risks to the coalition will ensue when these partners are assigned roles beyond the level of their capabilities, or if undue political and economic stress is placed on them to bring their technology up to par. This is a self-induced vulnerability that could easily become a weak link in coalition operations. In most cases, these partners could be placed in roles commensurate with their level of capability and still be integrated into the overall operation. Indeed, even within the four nations supporting this study, meaningful differences exist in the budgets available to support new technologies and the capability to take advantage of newly emerging commercial systems and approaches.
- Disparate measures of protecting C^4 assets pose yet another risk since, if known to the adversary, they can focus their efforts on these

vulnerable nodes, thereby obtaining a detrimental effect on the entire coalition network. Moreover, the use of commercial technology in coalition C^4 assets provides many advantages, but also creates vulnerabilities. Such technology can easily be acquired and analyzed by adversaries and later manipulated both physically and electronically.

Coalitions, even alliances, have found the creation of interoperable systems slow going. It took almost a year of the SACEUR's personal time to form the 36 nation coalition that went into Bosnia in December 1995. Most of the time was spent discussing cooperability issues of what forces would report to whom, how the nation would be involved in decision-making, and who could direct forces (and who could not) in combat. Interoperability issues were not dealt with fully until forces were on the ground. A quick look at Kosovo reveals the same level of effort and the continued existence of the same cooperability issues, although there are also serious technology issues in Kosovo, such as aircraft limitations and air control problems, that were not addressed in Bosnia.

As already noted in chapter two, cultural biases have tended to become imbedded in threat analysis, at least partly because coalition partners do not share a common method for converting threat data to information. This creates another form of analytical or cognitive interoperability that needs to be addressed.

In addition, as the brief review of NATO efforts to improve technical interoperability indicates, the formal alliances are sometimes unlikely to generate progress fast enough to keep up with or take advantage of rapidly improving technologies. NATO's efforts must be carried out within a structure that demands cooperation from all the members. Moreover, fiscal constraints are real.

FUTURE INTEROPERABILITY: LIKELY RISKS, IMPROVEMENTS, AND IMPEDIMENTS

Mission Success
Improved mission success is the bottom line for enhanced interoperability and cooperability. Recent operations in Bosnia and Kosovo have demonstrated both the need for better linkages between the national forces involved in coalition operations and the benefits arising from a more shared understanding of the situation, more integrated planning, and better coordinated execution. However, they have also demonstrated the limits of existing approaches and technology. These include delays in bringing C^4ISR capability into a richly integrated system, differences in doctrine and procedures when working with those who do not have the benefit of NATO experience and agreements, problems when NATO and other coalition agreements are

followed selectively, and the need to rely on one coalition partner for much of the key technology; all show how much room remains for improvement.

Coalition Continuity and Cohesion
The relatively low risk operations with stand-off weapons demonstrated in Kosovo have considerable potential for military effectiveness and make it easier to achieve and maintain coalition cohesion. At the same time, strategic level decisions such as the ROE to be used, the types of targets to be struck, and the degree of risk to be accepted during operations forced lengthy discussions and impacted military performance. Given that the will exists to build and maintain coalitions, generating prior agreement on key issues such as a common approach to operational planning within combined staffs, common ROE, military missions, and key contingencies that can be foreseen, will all need attention if prompt and effective guidance is to be provided to coalition forces.

Information Security
Coalition cohesion and effectiveness depend upon achieving and maintaining a high degree of shared awareness and the ability to utilize all available information. Current inabilities to exchange information among allies and coalition partners have hampered recent operations.

Coalitions often find themselves relying on the lowest common denominator for their C^4ISR systems. Moreover, when those most closely engaged in military situations, the "pointy end of the spear", are also among the technologically disadvantaged members of the coalition, the operators have a tendency to ignore or pay lip service to dissemination guidelines. Reports from both Bosnia and Kosovo indicate that these practices resulted in compromises that placed forces at risk. In theory they could have placed the missions at risk. Hence, the need for secure and assured interoperability and cooperability are clear to the working group. This problem may be worse when the full need to cooperate with non-military actors is recognized.

A major obstacle to the exchange of information has been the lack of an accepted method of achieving multi-level security (MLS). Recent advances in technology present an opportunity for the four powers to make progress in that area. A traditional sticking point has been the view that, somehow, a "silver bullet" technical solution guaranteeing security would be developed. The working group did not consider this likely in the foreseeable future, largely because of policy issues.

Risk management, as opposed to risk avoidance, is the logic that the study group recognized as likely to generate coalition agreement and solutions. The concept development and experimentation (CDE) effort is currently exploring alternative tools and approaches consistent with this philosophy.

THE NEED FOR EMPIRICAL EXPERIMENTATION

Demonstrating the effects of improved interoperability and cooperability is, in fact, an excellent candidate for experimental analysis. A very simple analytic design, which will arise as a natural experiment when different groups of potential coalition partners are exercising together, would serve to document the improvement. Allies frequently conduct both command post and field exercises. The exercises normally follow national education and training with the aim to support joint and combined operations. Less formal coalitions tend to do so on a bilateral basis, as general preparations for new mission types such as peace support operations or humanitarian assistance, or when they perceive a likely mission. Properly organized and instrumented, these exercises provide a venue for measuring the impact of different levels and types of interoperability and cooperability. Exercises involving unusual couplings of military establishments or other actors can also be used to establish a baseline for their absence.

There are two activities that represent opportunities to leverage ongoing efforts; Advanced Concept Technology Demonstrations (ACTD's) and the CFBL. ACTD's, a keystone of acquisition reform, involve warfighters as equal partners at initiation, and provide them with an assessment of military utility before, rather than after, acquisition. This saves money and time by identifying immature technology before large, expensive formal acquisition programs are started. For those technologies that receive positive evaluation, the concepts of operation (CONOPS) and tactics, techniques and procedures (TTP's) evolve with the new technology capability. This speeds up and enhances utility to the warfighter. By supporting new capabilities in operational hands for two years after the final military utility assessment, ACTD's get successful technology, CONOPS and TTP's to warfighters faster. Currently, about thirty percent of ACTD's have foreign participation.

The CFBL facilitates multi national C^4ISR interoperability, integration, research, and development activities identified by U.S. theater CINC's, and supports the Joint Chiefs-of-Staff Chairman's Joint Vision 2010. CFBL provides a centralized, full time, near real-time environment whereby the U.S. and coalition partners can investigate new and emerging technologies, conduct experimentation, and develop concepts of operation for the sharing of information across coalition boundaries. Current participants include the United States, United Kingdom, NC^3A (representing NATO), Canada, Australia, and New Zealand.

A program of experimentation would, however, require agreement that data be collected in exercises in which the problems (scenarios) and coalitions are of roughly equal complexity, the missions similar, and the "pace of battle" (or decision-making required) comparable, but with meaningfully different levels of interoperability. Alternatively, two or more components involved in the same exercise could operate with different levels of cooperability and interoperability. For more detailed examination of the dynamics at work, special command post exercises could be designed in facilities such as the Warrior Preparation Center, or in exercise and training centers of national colleges where experimental or exercise control and better instrumentation would be available. By using a variety of commanders and staffs, norms for performance of C^2 systems and force effectiveness could also be established and the impact of improved interoperability and cooperability measured.

Undertaking a campaign of experimentation focused on coalition interoperability and cooperability would provide the participating governments, and the larger community of potential partners, with tangible measures and evidence of the benefits that can be expected from investments. This can be expected to result in more efforts in this arena that would build on the early work, and also to result in improved "real world" operations because the exercises will directly enhance both practical interoperability and the key human elements of cooperability. Differences in organization, doctrine, training, concepts of operation, and other factors for the enhancement of interoperability and cooperability will arise naturally and will have to be dealt with in order to complete the exercises. Conducting such an experimental campaign will also force the policy makers in the governments involved to think through the difficult policy issues, such as what they are willing to share during coalition operations, in terms of systems capabilities as well as information Commanders and staffs will be exposed to one another and will find ways to synchronize and coordinate. Such experience in working together is often the key to improved coalition cooperation and effectiveness.

FINDINGS

- The four nations need to shift their focus from an almost exclusive one on technical interoperability to a balanced treatment of the technical, cognitive, organizational and doctrinal aspects of interoperability and cooperability.

- The four nations need to baseline current interoperability and cooperability characteristics and mission shortfalls to serve as a point of departure for efforts to explore the nature of improvements in this area.

- Since retrofitting interoperability is often slow and expensive, the four nations would be better off cooperating in the research, development, and acquisition phases of coalition C^4ISR systems, doctrine, and procedures.

- Recent advances, when coupled with risk management approaches to MLS such as those being explored by CDE, should provide adequate information security.

DEVELOPMENT OBJECTIVES

- The four nations represented in this working group should encourage cooperation in C^{4}ISR research, development, and acquisition of systems, doctrine, and procedures for coalition operations.

- The four nations should build on existing efforts at bilateral, allied, and multi-lateral interoperability and extend them from narrow technical interoperability tests to include issues of cooperability.

- Overall, an experimental program should be initiated, using different levels of complexity and reality (wargames, simulations, command post exercises, and true lessons learned efforts) to build systematic and empirical knowledge about what works in coalition operations. Experimentation should be conceived and conducted in a pragmatic manner that focuses on the relevance of information, its timely transmission, and ways to leverage this information.

- The four nations should pursue a risk management approach (*vice* risk avoidance) to MLS as part of future four power or coalition experiments.

IV. TECHNOLOGY: OPPORTUNITIES AND CONCERNS

War is a product of its age. The tools and tactics of how we fight have always evolved along with technology. This trend will continue, and warfare in the information age will inevitably embody the characteristics that distinguish this age from previous ones. These characteristics affect the capabilities that are brought to battle as well as the nature of the environment in which conflicts occur. Often in the past, military organizations pioneered both the development of technology and its application. Such is not the case today. Major advances in information technology are being driven primarily by the demands of the commercial sector.

Information technology is being applied commercially in ways that are transforming business around the globe. Virtual organizations, collaborative environments, and better informed decision-making are creating new benchmarks of performance. Both the relationships among individuals within organizations and those among organizations themselves are evolving as a result of information- and communication-related capabilities. Similar ideas and practices are beginning to take root in military thinking, concepts, plans, and experiments. This chapter begins with a brief discussion that highlights a number of the significant technology trends as well as the opportunities and challenges they present. The chapter explores the implications for interoperability and military capabilities, concluding with a set of recommendations.

TECHNOLOGY TRENDS, OPPORTUNITIES & CHALLENGES

Dramatic increases in processing power are at the heart of the information revolution. Moore's Law describes an exponential increase in processing power (a doubling of processing power every 18 months) that shows no sign of abating for the next ten years. Communications bandwidth is growing even faster. In other words, our ability to process and share information has grown and continues to grow at astonishing rates.

This vastly increased ability to process and communicate information has motivated new generations of information related capabilities and tools, such as data mining, visualization, and collaboration environments. These capabilities and tools are designed to enable the exploitation of this vastly increased availability of information as well as the ability to share it with others.

The opportunities abound. Increasingly potent information-related capabilities are becoming available at ever decreasing costs. Only imagination and ability to overcome institutional inertia bound the potential of an information driven revolution in military affairs. But make no mistake, the opportunities associated with the information age are accompanied by a set of challenges that could, if not adequately met, make technologically advanced nations worse off than before by threatening them with an unmanageable information overload, by eroding their existing information edge over potential adversaries, and by exposing them to new vulnerabilities.

As world class technology becomes more widely available in the form of commercial-off-the-shelf (COTS) products and dramatically decreased cost to performance ratios, even non-state actors can afford significant capability. To make matters worse, "last generation" equipment, which not too long ago was responsible for creating a military advantage for advanced nations, is currently available on the open market for a very small fraction of its original cost. Greatly increased inter-connectivity and increased reliance on the ability to collect, process, and disseminate information on and off the battlefield also result in increased vulnerability.

Figure 4, "How Information Concepts Alter the Landscape", depicts the way in which information age technologies are influencing and shaping the National Security Environment.

Figure 4: How Information Age Concepts Alter the Landscape

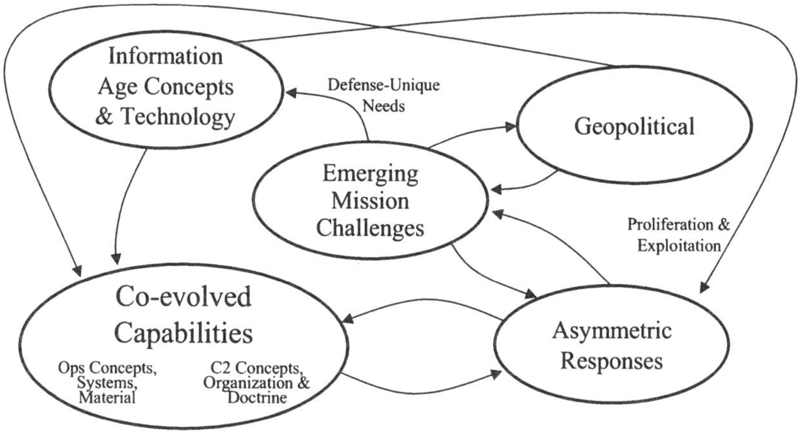

Information age concepts and technologies affect the ability to detect, track, and identify targets, the ability to share information across the joint operations arena, and the capacity to act on that shared information. This in turn directly affects the nature of the **co-evolved capabilities** and outcomes, including the time it takes to be in a position to respond to a threat or action, the precision with which a particular target can be struck, and the expected number of casualties associated with a given operation. As military capability improves, **asymmetrical responses** may be spawned as adversaries attempt directly to counter the technology related effectiveness of new military capabilities or to render these new capabilities politically or militarily useless. As asymmetric responses emerge, enabled in part by widely available COTS technology, the **emerging mission challenges** faced by technologically advanced militaries increase and create new defense-unique needs. The shifting balance of capabilities has an influence on the **geopolitical situation**, which in turn affects the **emerging mission challenges** faced by militaries. As **asymmetric responses** are developed and as emerging mission challenges evolve over time, militaries will need to continue to co-evolve their operational capabilities to respond.

IMPACT ON INTEROPERABILITY

Advances in information technology and the dynamics of the situation described above will affect the ability of militaries to interoperate in both positive and negative ways. On the positive side, the market place creation of de facto technical standards to support the commercial sector, the continued pressures of globalization, the lower costs of basic capabilities, and the progress in collaborative environments and artificial intelligence applications (including translation) will make it easier for organizations to exchange information and to collaborate if there is a will to do so. But differences in the rates at which organizations acquire and assimilate new technologies and their different cultural approaches to organizational and C^2 issues will make cooperability more challenging to achieve. These organizational and C^2 issues include the allocation of responsibilities within organizations, the distribution of information, and the automation of decision processes.

Thus, while advancing technology and its widespread availability and affordability will make it easier to achieve technical interoperability, and to a lesser extent semantic or cognitive interoperability, the achievement of cooperability will be far more difficult. The tendency to wait for technological solutions to problems involving interoperability and security is misguided. There are, in fact, no technological "magic bullets". Furthermore, an integrated approach to interoperability and security is of particular importance, since effective interoperability depends upon finding ways to solve the persistent "multi-level" security problem and to achieve an adequate level of information assurance. Thus, achieving desirable levels of interoperability and cooperability needs to begin with the capabilities that technologies provide and build upon them, weaving these capabilities into a comprehensive approach.

The answer thus can be found in the development of balanced, coherent mission capability packages.[9] Such packages can result only from a process that encourages innovation and facilitates co-evolution. As indicated earlier, experimentation[10] is an essential part of the process of discovery, exploration, testing, assessment, and demonstration that are the engines of co-evolution. Because of an imperfect understanding of multi-cultural cognitive processes and the complexity of the interactions involved in achieving cooperability, systematic experimentation must be a mainstay of the journey to the future.

IMPEDIMENTS TO PROGRESS

Significant obstacles need to be overcome to achieve enhanced coalition interoperability and cooperability. Some of these, such as differences in the way militaries adapt to the information age, differences in language and in organizational cultures, the enormous complexity of confederations of systems, and the relative ability of different actors to afford state-of-the-art technologies, have been previously mentioned. One must add to these the heavy burden exerted by legacy systems and the existing stovepipes that separate intelligence from CIS systems. Finally, and perhaps most importantly, there is a lack of a shared vision of how militaries could or should work together in the future.

The proliferation of systems presents a challenge of increasing complexity. The need to filter and process large volumes of information from disparate sources, the large and often unpredictable ways information is disseminated within organizations, the complexities associated with the behavior of distributed entities, and, in the case of coalitions, the complexities introduced by differences in culture and language, all combine to create a level of complexity not previously experienced. This level of complexity can not be adequately dealt with by top-down efforts to restrict information or choice, but needs to be better understood through research, experimentation, and practice. The risks associated with increased complexity cannot be mitigated by forced simplicity, but by emphasizing an approach that stresses robustness, flexibility, and adaptability.

The ad hoc nature of the coalitions formed to meet mission challenges in the last decade of the 20th century have certainly provided a wealth of experience on what works and what does not, and could provide a good point of departure for the exploration of future coalition arrangements. Developing a common understanding of future capabilities that can be expected from the commercial sector is essential for progress. Of particular interest is the nature of the security guarantees that will accompany future

---

[9] See Chapter 3 for further discussion of Mission Capability Packages.
[10] Read Richard E. Hayes, "Experimentation Typology", Appendix C.

Technology: Opportunities and Concerns

commercial products and services. Exactly how militaries can make use of civilian infrastructure and issues of availability and security during crises and conflicts remains of paramount concern.

The related issue of critical infrastructure protection (CIP) is quickly moving to the top of a list of concerns related to asymmetric responses. How can coalition partners work together to protect their own and each others critical infrastructures upon which the coalition depends? Given the degree of interconnectivity of communications infrastructures (just to mention one), it will take an integrated or a coordinated effort at the very least to monitor performance, detect anomalies, assess damage, and respond coherently. Thus, it will take a coalition effort just to ensure the ability to mount successfully a coalition operation able to take advantage of information age technologies and the processes that they empower.

FINDINGS

- Technological change, largely occurring in information technology, is altering the need and potential for coalition C^4ISR in profound ways.

- Given the rates of technological dissemination and exploitation in the world, coalitions will ignore those changes only at the peril of being unable to achieve their purposes.

- Commercial technologies, standards, and practices will affect the potential for coalition C^4ISR technologies, as well as their limits. Commercial practice will show what is possible, commercial standards will have a profound impact on the degree of technical interoperability possible, and the security of commercial information technologies will determine their suitability and availability for coalition military applications.

DEVELOPMENT OBJECTIVES

- Adopt a Mission Capability Package framework to ensure the co-evolution of operational concepts, command approaches, organizations, doctrine, and systems.

- Employ a program of allied and coalition experimentation[11] to explore mutually new concepts and technologies to:
  - contribute to a better understanding of the implications of the information age;

---

[11] See Richard E. Hayes, "Potential Coalition Experiments", Appendix D.

- move towards a common vision of future interoperability/cooperability; and
- incrementally build confidence in our understanding of the problem and the solutions.

• Use experimentation to explore risk management approaches to information sharing and security.

• Capitalize on existing laboratories, networks, research networks and planned experiments where possible.

• Undertake research in the following areas:
  - the relationship between technology and asymmetric responses;
  - modeling asymmetric conflicts (performance testing); and
  - the nature of complex systems and approaches to testing, security, etc.[12]

• Adopt a confederated approach to building the "system of systems" that will support coalition operations.

• Base interoperability on an open systems architecture and de facto marketplace standards to the greatest extent possible, adding the military unique requirement only when essential.

• Establish a permanent "lessons learned" activity to focus on coalition interoperability.

• Focus on achieving shared awareness, first addressing the cognitive level of cooperability and then tackling the interoperability related impediments to capitalizing on this to achieve improved unity of effort (synchronization).

• Undertake a program to assist military officers better to understand emerging technologies and their significance.

---

[12] Read Uwe Wiemken, "Complexity", Appendix E.

V. ORGANIZATIONAL ISSUES

WHY EXAMINE ORGANIZATIONAL ISSUES

C^2 interoperability and cooperability require far more than the ability to exchange information among the CIS or information systems of the coalition partners. They also require a degree of organizational coherence and compatibility. The organizational issues relevant to the three classes of coalition operations identified earlier in this report include how the military forces of the participating nations interface with one another, their link to the other actors relevant to coalition missions,[13] and the functional relationships by which logistics, communications, and other services are to be provided.

The variety of organizational issues and the relevant solutions suggest the term "command arrangements" is more appropriate than the classic "command and control" when military operations other than war (MOOTW) are conducted.[14] The term "command arrangements" recognizes that military forces within coalitions will only take direct orders to the extent that they are consistent with the agreements made by their governments, and that other actors such as international organizations and non-governmental organizations cannot be given orders at all, but rather must be persuaded to cooperate with military organizations.

Organizational forms should be matched to the type of mission assigned. In other words, no single organizational type should be presumed to be ideal for war fighting and peace operations. Moreover, the suitability of organizational forms is partly dependent on the technological capabilities possessed by members of the coalition with respect to communications, data collection and processing, information handling, and the exchange of knowledge. As information technologies have developed and their applications matured, commercial practice has demonstrated structural change in the form of a flattening of organizations, and functional change through the elimination of some functions and the integration of others. This commercial evolution is suggestive of changes that can be anticipated in military coalitions. The working group developed a series of questions about organizational issues in the context of C^4ISR. Those questions and responses to them can be found on the project web site.

---

[13] As previously noted in this report, such actors include host governments, non-governmental organizations, private volunteer organizations, and international organizations.

[14] David S. Alberts and Richard E. Hayes, *Command Arrangements for Peace Operations* (Washington, D.C.: National Defense University Press, May 1995).

ORGANIZATIONAL EXPERIENCE AND PRACTICES

Coalitions have adopted four traditional approaches to deal with organizational issues. These practices are not new. They were employed on ancient battlefields as well as during World War II. By and large, the same tools have been used within national forces, in formal alliances, and within coalitions. They remain useful today and can be expected as part of the organizational approaches to be employed in the three classes of operations of interest to the working group. Those tools include:

- geographic separation;
- functional separation;
- liaison teams; and
- combined headquarters.

First, different geographic areas have been assigned to different national forces or to forces with different capabilities. For example, on ancient battlefields, the "irregular" forces were physically separated from the line forces, often in locations where their performance would not decide the battle. NATO's war plans during the Cold War also assigned physically distinct geographic regions to the ground forces from different nations, thus simplifying issues of C^2.

Second, different missions or functions are typically assigned to coalition forces with different capabilities. NATO mine countermeasures are assigned to the most capable forces, not distributed equally across national navies. Similarly, those nations with better night and all weather flying capabilities were assigned missions during the 1991 Gulf War that employed those capabilities to best coalition advantage.

These first two approaches are often employed together. For example, the light French armor was assigned a screening role on the western flank during the Gulf War to ensure a meaningful mission without undue risk to that force. This was both a geographic "control feature" that simplified coalition C^2 and also an intelligent military use of a capable, specialized force.

Third, coalition partners have traditionally exchanged liaison officers. This practice began in antiquity as a way to improve cooperability. Even equally capable and similar forces from different nations and military traditions must make a conscious effort to understand one another's doctrines and practices. Liaison officers also provide a mechanism for improving communication about the military situation. As technological differences have developed, they have also proven invaluable as a way to link more and less capable forces. In modern times, these liaison forces may include, for example, communications systems not available to the less capable force, as was the case with U.S. special forces teams assigned to Syria during *Desert Storm*. U.S. forces in Somalia had a separate intelligence cell that shared selected products with coalition partners. Liaison teams have the advantage of allowing discussion of potential missions and the support they require, such as desired lead time and assets, as early in the planning process as possible. They also reduce the chance of cultural misunderstandings between coalition partners.

Finally, combined headquarters have been developed for many coalition forces. These typically involve national "balance" among key personnel and roles, and their creation is often the topic of intense debate among the participating nations. Combined headquarters may also sit atop military organizations that are assigned physically separate geographic or functional commands nation. The classic example of a modern combined headquarters was Eisenhower's for *Operation Overlord*, which was also the model for the UN in the Korean Conflict. This has, of course, been the approach taken in NATO and UN peace operations as well as with the warfighting coalition in *Desert Storm*. The NATO concept of a CJTF as the key military organization for future missions is building on this practice.

THE LIMITS OF TRADITIONAL APPROACHES

Unfortunately, the demands of modern combat render these traditional solutions ineffective by themselves. Geographic organization, for example, has proven inadequate in the arenas of air defense and offensive air operations. The areas occupied by the ground forces of a single nation, whether brigade, division, corps, or even army corps, can be overflown so quickly by fixed wing air, attacked by rotary wing aircraft from adjacent zones, and struck by rockets or missiles from beyond their own areas of interest and responsibility so readily, that they cannot defend their forces locally. Hence, alliances such as NATO and military coalitions have created integrated air tasking orders, coalition wide C^2 systems to control air operations, and the associated doctrines, tactics, procedures, and techniques to integrate their air defenses and air operations into a centralized structure. Geographic separation simply does not make sense in this arena.

Looking into the future, geographic separation of ground and naval forces will also make less and less sense. First, the air threat will force increasingly closer cooperation and more attention to geographic "seams" as vulnerabilities. These seams have also been a traditional target for military forces as well as a focal point for coordination between and among coalition partners. In an information age where creating a common operational picture is crucial, sharing of information from all sources and sectors becomes even more important. Assignment of distinct geographic sectors will tend to perpetuate the practice of sending locally collected information up the national chain of command for processing before it is provided to coalition partners. This practice creates a source of difference in data and information among partners due to the delays incurred, and is also vulnerable to activities conducted "just over the boundary" and therefore out of sight.

Second, the speed of land and naval combat is also increasing. Forces massed, even briefly, present targets for weapons of mass effects if the mass can be foreseen or detected quickly enough. The ability to employ stand-off weapons and to exploit emerging network technologies (sensor to shooter, for example) also depends on rapid reaction as well as synchronization between different elements of the force.

Functional separation will also be less useful in the future, although budgetary pressures will continue to argue for different nations to develop unique capabilities, such as mine countermeasures, all weather aircraft, stealth technology, and specialized sensors. However, coalitions must more tightly integrate those unique capabilities into overall plans in order to take advantage of them to conduct more effective operations. For example, mine sweeping cannot be conducted efficiently or effectively while under active attack, so security will need to be established to apply this specialized force to the advantage of the coalition. Similarly, specialized sensors must be integrated into a coalition's intelligence tasking, collection, and analysis plan to be of value.

Logistics often represent a unique challenge in coalition operations, which have handled them by variations on the functional separation theme. Alternative arrangements have included national provision, host country provision, and provision by some well endowed coalition members to others. Clearly, national provision dominates when the forces are equipped differently. Equally clearly, host governments are expected to provide what they can. In coalitions established to provide international legitimacy, the better endowed countries often provide equipment, transportation, and sustainment to the less well endowed countries' forces. In modern coalitions, logistics coordination has become a major enterprise. Given improving information systems, increasing integration of these very specialized capabilities will also be essential.

Hence, while *specialization* can be expected to continue and even increase in coalition operations, *functional separation* will become less and less practical and more of a barrier to efficiency and military effectiveness. This trend is even stronger in MOOTW missions, where support and specialized capabilities will often extend to non-military goods and services such as the provision of shelter and food, and to providing "dual use" services such as communications and transportation to non-military organizations and civilian populations. Examples of this specialization include assigning one nation the mission of protecting a building and another nation the use of rockets or missiles to protect coalition forces and another nation the theater air defense mission.

Liaison teams will continue to be quite important in future coalition operations, particularly where some partners do not possess highly capable military forces. First, these teams can provide communications using systems that might not be shareable with some countries' militaries, such as the cases of Syria in *Desert Storm* or Russia in the Kosovo peacekeeping force. Non-military organizations, for example, host governments or the UN, could also be the recipients of these services. Second, liaison teams can act as filters for the exchange of information consistent with national dissemination policies, as the U.S. intelligence cell did in Somalia.

Perhaps more important, they provide cultural linkages - bridging differences of language, doctrine, and world view. The creation of civil-military cooperation divisions of task forces designed to work with non-military organizations in MOOTW's is a crucial structural change that essentially creates specialized liaison offices for coordination across cultural (both national and organizational) boundaries.

The inherent limitations of liaison teams, however, are lack of speed and lack of genuine access and participation in decision-making. They are too slow to coordinate execution of operations in the modern battle space. They depend on human interactions more suited to creating a common perception of the situation and planning rather than to execution. Almost by definition, they are also indirect. Liaison officers do not participate directly in decision-making, course of action analysis, or other crucial activities unless specifically invited by their host institutions. Even when they do participate, they are junior to the decision-makers in rank and "outsiders" within the organization. Hence, while valuable, they are not an adequate organizational mechanism for coalition C^2 integration, cooperability, and interoperability.

Coalition combined headquarters are intended to provide the venue where genuinely integrated perceptions, analyses, and decisions can take place. As noted earlier, the idea of NATO in creating and training CJTF's for this purpose is an effort to employ this tool to advantage to provide mobile operational level headquarters in future missions. Although CJTF's have been employed *de facto* in Bosnia and Kosovo, NATO members have yet to agree on the formal implementation of the concept. Even the U.S., which has developed its own JTF and CJTF doctrine and has led in creating the NATO concept, has found itself creating specialized command arrangements for each operation.

Coalition partners have historically created combined headquarters through a process of national negotiation rather than designing them for the optimum performance of a particular mission. Indeed, negotiations about the coalition headquarters often occur while the nations are debating the mission itself. One consequence of this ad hoc process has been that combined headquarters often change over time as the realities of the mission are encountered and "form" is altered to fit "function". Another consequence of this ad hoc process has been the creation of "strange" structures. For example, bringing Russia into the coalition for Bosnia involved the creation of reporting structures that ran from the forces on the ground to a Russian general officer at NATO headquarters, without passing through the NATO commander in the theater. The NATO Joint Analysis Team (JAT) for Bosnia pointed out a number of such organizational anomalies within the coalition, some involving long standing members of NATO.

Combined headquarters also imply the existence of a coherent system of military communications and information processing. While these systems have been created in the past, they have typically been more correctly understood as a conglomeration of systems that patch together national systems and selected locations through specialized or isolated circuits and networks (sometimes termed stovepipes), as well as through ad hoc linkages designed on the spot. Weeks, and often months, have passed before these linkages are put in place, even in operations as recent as Bosnia and Kosovo. Traditional approaches to creating these information processing and communications systems take too long and need to be replaced by approaches that will take advantage of modern technologies, such as those that permit a wide variety of users and applications to rely on the internet, and of collaborative tools for information processing and decision-making.

ORGANIZATIONAL FORMS AND CHARACTERISTICS

While organizations can be described in an almost infinite number of ways, the working group concluded that three dimensions were crucial for the purposes of its analysis:

- patterns of connectivity;
- distributions of authority and responsibility; and
- roles of participants.

Connectivity refers to the nodes and links of the organization. The number of nodes matters, as does the way they are connected and the robustness of the linkages. More nodes create greater burdens on communications, information processing, and dissemination, all other things being equal. Forms of connection include all nodes linked among themselves, hierarchies, and stove pipes for some information. While militaries have traditionally been hierarchies, their linkage systems are increasingly becoming networks, which has profound implications for decision-making and for operations.

Distribution of responsibility and authority deals with which activities occur at each node, the level of detail at which they are managed at each node, and the reporting relationships within the organization. For example, most military structures have broad responsibility at command nodes -

Organizational Issues

spanning traditional functions of personnel, intelligence, operations, logistics, plans, and communications. However, specialized structures also exist for fire direction, coordination with non-military organizations, and other functions. Moreover, some military organizations have adopted "skip-echelon" structures in which some functions are not robustly executed at all levels. For example, Israeli C^2 systems skip some echelons for logistics and personnel matters.

More typically, different military organizations will have doctrines that lead to greater or lesser degrees of centralization. Very centralized systems, such as NATO Air Tasking Orders, generate quite detailed orders from high in the structure, specifying what to do, where to do it, with which forces, and when. Very decentralized systems, on the other hand, try to generate "mission type" directives that permit the implementing commander great discretion in how to achieve the assigned mission. In between are structures that organize the central guidance around particular objectives and constraints. The emerging idea of network centric warfare assumes yet another distribution in which elements of the coalition are able to "self-synchronize" their activities. These different approaches to decision-making are based on very different distributions of authority and responsibility. As technology matures and enables choices among these distributions, coalitions will need to agree on consistent approaches.

Roles consist of the behaviors expected by "self" and by others in the organization. Military organizations typically have doctrinally defined roles for each node in their structures and for each key person within those nodes. Defining and practicing these roles, whether in exercises or operations, is crucial in order for the organization to avoid role overlap and role gaps. In role overlap, multiple parts of the organization spend time and energy issuing potentially different directives in a functional area, while role gaps result in necessary functions not being controlled by anyone or being handled disjointedly.

Coalitions, because they do not start with a common doctrine or set of practices, are prone to both role gaps and role overlaps, as well as to simple confusion about the particular roles of nodes and individuals within the structure. Hence, in the development of NATO's CJTF headquarters doctrine, considerable effort must and is being spent in defining roles within the CJTF headquarters, between the CJTF headquarters and the forces it commands, and between the CJTF headquarters and international organizations, non-governmental organizations, private volunteer organizations, and host governments. Considerable effort must also be expected in training commanders and staffs in those roles and in their proper implementation, as well as in establishing how the CJTF headquarters will generate adequate and efficient interoperability and cooperability with outside organizations.

Moreover, NATO is working to develop CJTF headquarters and corresponding C^2 structures for specific mission types.

MATCHING FORM TO MISSION

No one organizational form is ideal or optimal for all missions or purposes. Peter Drucker, for example, points out that, "there is no such thing as the one right organization".[15] He goes on to indicate, "the executive of the future will require a toolbox full of organizational structures", and offers the guidance that "mission defines strategy, after all, and strategy defines structure". This insight applies directly to military missions, at several levels.

First, as previously noted, those mission arenas such as air defense and air operations that require extraordinary speed of decision-making and execution, and that advanced technologies can support, are becoming increasingly centralized.

Second, different types of warfare are best conducted with different degrees of centralization. This argument, when extended to peace operations, implies that yet other structures, such as for civil-military cooperation, are required for these missions.

Third, research, extending from small group experimentation and systems dynamics to analyses of military exercises and operations, demonstrates tension between those structures that are capable of rapid decisions and those capable of making good quality decisions in complex situations. In general, the larger the number of participants and the greater their connectivity, the slower the decision-making. At the same time, more participants and greater capacity to exchange information and perspectives are associated with higher quality decisions in complex situations. Given that senior commanders in both combat and peace operations are faced with complex decisions in which the stakes are high, finding the correct balance for any given coalition and mission will be crucial. Indeed, one of the key implications of this research is that coalitions should stress contingency planning as a way of ensuring that difficult decisions are broadly discussed within the coalition as early as possible in order to avoid having to make complex decisions under time pressure.

THE NEED FOR EXPLORATORY EXPERIMENTATION

Given the large number of factors involved in organizational issues, the possible use of traditional approaches to mitigate them in coalitions, the pace of change and potential contributions of technology to coalition C^2, and the variety of missions coalitions may undertake, no simple solution will be

---

[15] *Forbes*, 5 October 1998.

found. Indeed, the working group remains convinced that no single solution for optimum coalition organization will emerge. Elegant theoretical solutions are doomed to fail in the face of practical needs and national interests. Ad hoc solutions, however, will continue to be plagued with both inefficiencies and the constant need for changes "on the fly" as political circumstances, coalition missions, and technologies change.

Hence, the working group concluded that a very real need exists for a campaign of exploratory experimentation in which promising organizational approaches are subjected to the rigors of simulations, war games, command post exercises and other environments where coalition partners can evaluate them. *Exploratory* experimentation is needed because the realm of potential organizational alternatives is simply too large to permit systematic examination, and because experimentation for formal hypothesis testing would require an unrealistic investment. *Experimentation* is needed because there is ample experience and evidence that the traditional approaches are less than ideal and will increasingly be inadequate over time, but there is also no systematic evidence of the value of alternative or novel approaches.

Empirical observation and measurement will be needed in order to establish the value of new approaches and to ensure that they have an impact on the key dimensions of decision-making quality, decision-making speed, and operational efficiency. An *experimental campaign* is needed because the problem is too complex to yield to a single effort and because the best hope of good quality solutions arises from cumulative learning and knowledge. In addition to exercises and evaluations, less formal settings such as seminars and wargames also provide opportunities to discuss deficiencies, and should be included in the experimentation process.

Finally, rather than jumping directly to command post exercises or relying wholly on them, the campaign should also include the following types of experiments:

- cost effective simulations of structural issues, for example, how much band-width is necessary for selected functions;
- war games that allow experts to identify organizational issues and suggest remedies; and
- reviews of coalition operations.

At the same time, the working group felt strongly that designing and implementing simple command post exercises would be an important part of the process. It will force the participating nations to deal with issues that would not be encountered in less realistic environments. These issues include, for example, what information to share, how to link nationally procured systems, or what command arrangements would be politically acceptable. Hence, command post exercises should be part of the original plan and should be scheduled as early as practical in the process.

FINDINGS

- Current organizational remedies to deal with the lack of C^2 interoperability and cooperability (geographic and functional separation, liaison teams, and combined headquarters) are not sufficient to deal with the new missions, new mission environments, and technological changes that coalitions are likely to deal with in the future.

- Not all technologically feasible organizational forms are either practical or desirable. Both cultural and economic factors need to be considered. Moreover, doctrinal issues may need to be resolved before some nations can find effective and efficient ways for their military establishments to work effectively together.
- There is no "one-size-fits-all" organizational solution that spans the set of anticipated missions and coalition partners. There are classes of approaches - degrees of centralization, designs for network operations and selfsynchronization, that can and should be explored.

DEVELOPMENT OBJECTIVES

- Undertake a campaign of exploratory experimentation to examine alternative organizational approaches.
    - This campaign should start with small experiments focused on selected aspects of interoperability and cooperability: shared awareness and efficient, coherent coalition planning and execution.
    - These initial, small experiments should involve the four nations represented in this study as well as appropriate civilian agencies from their nations, international organizations, non-governmental agencies, and private voluntary organizations.

- Initial hypotheses worthy of examination include:
    - improved information exchange can achieve better coalition C^2; and
    - collaborative work environments can improve coalition C^2.

VI. DOCTRINE AND CONCEPT DEVELOPMENT

WHAT DOCTRINE IS

Whatever consensus emerges from multi-national deliberations and experimentation programs will be operationalized through the medium of doctrine. Doctrine is what is taught. It "is what warriors believe in and act on".[16] "It represents the central beliefs for waging war in order to achieve victory.... It is fundamental to sound judgement".[17] It "offers a common perspective from which to plan and operate, and fundamentally shapes the way we think about and train for war".[18]

The NATO definition of doctrine is "Fundamental principles by which the military forces guide their actions in support of objectives. It is authoritative but requires judgement in application". The principles and tenets of doctrine take into account all of the basic elements of a military force: weapon systems; information systems; levels of skill, experience and training at the individual, unit, and force level; deployment and sustainment capabilities; organizational issues; command and control philosophy and issues; and command arrangements for dealing with those outside the coalition.

Figure 5 shows the place of doctrine and its implications within the process of developing concepts for future operations, establishing requirements, acquiring capabilities, and conducting operations. Doctrine is distinguished from future concepts in that it is based on extant capabilities.

Where currently agreed doctrine is found to be inadequate in a changing operational environment, experimental doctrine may be produced. As a result of experiments and selective operational use, this experimental doctrine may become part of the agreed corpus of doctrine. It may expose shortfalls in capability which will entail procurement of new systems. Doctrine is therefore indirectly linked to the process of acquisition. On the one hand, the choice of equipment to be purchased is influenced by military planners, the threats they anticipate, and the concepts of operation they envisage using. On the other hand, at any given time the equipment in the inventory strongly influences the doctrine for employing forces.

---

[16] Wayne Hughes, Captain USN (Ret.), Fleet Tactics. U.S. Joint Publication 1. Joint Warfare of the U.S. Armed Forces (11/11/91). National Defense University Press.

[17] General Curtis LeMay, USAF, and a practitioner of coalition warfare during World War II. U.S. Joint Publication 1. Joint Warfare of the U.S. Armed Forces (11/11/91). National Defense University Press.

[18] U.S. Joint Publication 1. Joint Warfare of the US Armed Forces (11/11/95). National Defense University Press.

Figure 5: The Concepts/Operations Relationship

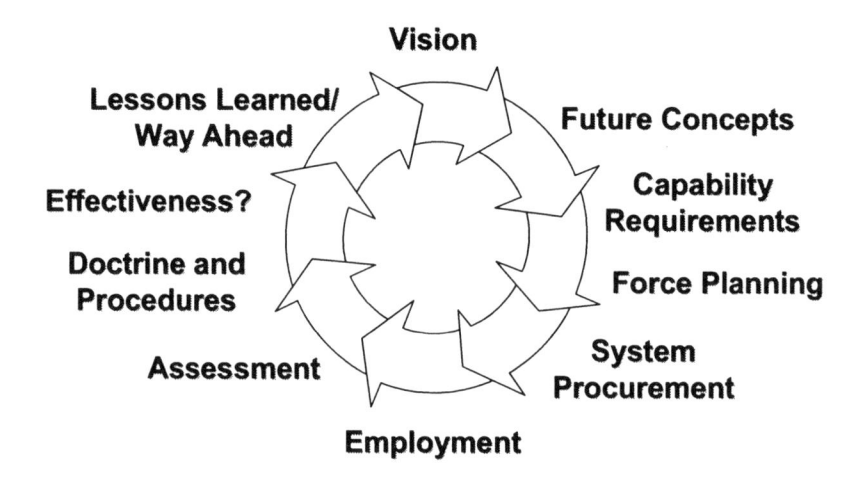

- Vision
- Future Concepts
- Capability Requirements
- Force Planning
- System Procurement
- Employment
- Assessment
- Doctrine and Procedures
- Effectiveness?
- Lessons Learned/Way Ahead

Doctrine is not about what is to be done, but about how it is to be accomplished. National or coalition strategic objectives define the goals of the enterprise. They are often influenced by senior military commanders, but grand strategic objectives are ultimately the responsibility of political authorities. National and coalition military commanders also have an important role in defining military objectives, which can best be understood as the effects the military are expected to create in their operating environment. Effective coalitions have coherent sets of strategic objectives, including military objectives, but these statements do not constitute doctrinal statements.

Doctrine is neither strategy[19] nor policy, though it often influences and is influenced by both. Doctrine is general, not particular. For example, Soviet Cold War land warfare doctrine told commanders to probe enemy defenses at multiple points and to launch heavy attacks at those places where weakness was detected. Field commanders were left free to make decisions about where to probe. They were responsible for deciding how they would recognize weakness, and distinguish it from deception designed to invite attacks where the enemy preferred to fight. These were tactical and operational decisions

---

[19] Grand strategy may be defined as the art and science of developing and using political, economic, psychological, and military forces as necessary during peace and war, to afford the maximum support to policies, in order to increase the probabilities and favorable consequences of victory and lessen the chances of defeat (U.S. Department of Defense Definition). Military strategy is "The art and science of employing the armed forces of a nation to secure the objectives of national policy by the application of force or the threat of force".

that depended on the assigned missions, terrain, weather, and forces available to both sides.

WHY IS DOCTRINE IMPORTANT FOR COALITIONS?

Why aspire to a corpus of common doctrine? The growing corpus of lessons learned about coalition operations is replete with examples of mistakes, missed opportunities, and even tragedies that can be traced to different countries' forces not doing things the same way or to one nation's military not knowing what to expect from another's.

A reasonable approach to such challenges is to prioritize, set realistic goals, and to maintain open communications. It must also be realized that there will always be legacy systems and dissimilar partners. There will always be variations in technological capabilities and differing national interests. Doctrinal harmonization and trust developed through ongoing exercises, experiments and dialogue among likely coalition partners can help overcome these inherent challenges.

The essence of doctrine is to establish the best common ways of employing military forces. Coalition doctrine establishes the best common ways of employing the military forces of multiple nations - the best ways of doing things that need to be done together. When agreed and published, doctrine facilitates the development of operational plans, the modification of organizations, the setting of resource priorities, and the formulation of training and exercising objectives. Areas where the role of doctrine is especially critical include coalition methods for: intelligence; C^2; communications; rapid deployment; force protection; rules of engagement; land operations; air, air defense and airspace operations; naval operations; logistic sustainment; and civil-military cooperation (CIMIC).

Coalition partners working with very different doctrines will obviously have problems harmonizing their efforts. Indeed, regardless of the degree of technical interoperability they might achieve, genuine cooperability will be all but impossible to achieve. In simplest terms, forces that operate on different fundamental principles become vulnerable to misunderstandings, poorly coordinated actions, and even working at cross-purposes. Doctrine can, if harmonized, be the glue of coalition operations. Finding ways to harmonize doctrine is, therefore, a priority effort to ensure improved coalition operations.

Doctrinal development remains a predominantly national responsibility. Each of the four countries represented in the working group is pursuing doctrine development via its own methodologies. These efforts are, however, influenced in the main by the same outside forces discussed in chapter one of this report. Given these common external factors, similar doctrinal priorities and responses should follow. However, this conclusion only goes so far. Nations often view threats differently, both in terms of risk and severity or even probability of occurrence. These differences contribute to interoperability challenges and must be thoroughly examined in order to enable cooperability.

Since doctrine pervades almost every element of the employment of military forces, and since any difference is a possible source of problems, adopting purely common doctrine would appear to be the only way to avoid problems. However, that is a time consuming and difficult process, as the NATO doctrine development effort has demonstrated. Nations have different force structures, cultures, military experiences, resources available for their military establishments, and perceptions of the threats that must be defeated.

Doctrinal divergence is likely in part to be the result of differences in national policy and strategy. Of the nations represented in this study, the United States, France and the United Kingdom have essentially adopted expeditionary strategic concepts in which the requirement to intervene at distance from the homeland is central. Germany is in the process of reconsidering a strategic concept that has been focused on territorial defense in the context of NATO.

Germany and the United Kingdom have customarily placed greater emphasis on NATO products in the form of tactics, techniques and procedures. With the reemergence of doctrine as an important military intellectual activity from the mid-1980's Germany and the United Kingdom are predisposed to the view that NATO should be the ultimate repository for common doctrine where the subject matter lies within the scope of NATO. As this scope is itself changing, it follows that NATO's responsibility for developing common doctrine should also be expanding. Germany and the United Kingdom would also tend to the view that in those subject areas where there is good NATO doctrine, there should be no need to have parallel national doctrine. The United States and France have generally inclined to the view that there is national doctrine, there is NATO doctrine, and that these should be harmonized but will never be identical.

There are also differences between nations in their general doctrinal approach to the use of military force. Germany's defensive predisposition has already been mentioned. France and the UK have, alongside their emphasis on expeditionary operations, adopted a manoeuverist approach at least to warfighting. This approach emphasizes the disruption of enemy fighting capability by the use of tempo and synchronization of effort to concentrate force in decisive events, involving in particular the targeting of nodes of vulnerability.

The UK attempts to apply the principles of the manoeuverist approach to all uses of military force, including peace operations. French doctrine distinguishes peace operations as an essentially different mode in which

Doctrine and Concept Development

military force is applied with the objective of "mastering violence". In practice, UK doctrine for peace operations - and the UK is lead nation in NATO for the development of this doctrine - is not essentially dissimilar to that of France.

It is important to note, however, that there are significant differences among nations in their doctrinal approach to peace operations in addition to the issue of protection discussed below. France, the UK, and the U.S. all acknowledge the important role of the appropriate use of force in achieving inducement in the context both of peacekeeping and peace enforcement. There is a doctrinal school[20] that emphasizes the theory of the "cycle of violence", and that includes many nations with considerable experience in peacekeeping. This theory asserts that an intervening coalition's use of force to achieve inducement will increase the propensity for potential belligerent factions to resort to violence, which will in turn demand a more aggressive posture by the peace support forces. These differences are expressed not only in the behavior of forces but also in the way that nations equip their forces and in the choice of missions and roles to which they will elect to commit them.

The crucial issue is how national doctrines actually differ with respect to coalition operations, particularly in the three types of situations of interest to this study: regional conflict, peace enforcement, and peacekeeping. U.S. doctrine stresses movement away from platform centric warfare towards network centric warfare. The UK has declared a general intent to move in the same direction, and NATO doctrine may also over time. However, no country has the resources to keep up with the U.S. in this endeavor over the next decade. Moreover, other potential coalition partners, of which France is one, are concerned about moving too far into automating the battlespace, and as a consequence developing technological dependencies that may either increase vulnerability to information warfare attacks or simply create machine driven systems that reduce the flexibility of commanders to practice the art of war.[21] Indeed, network centric warfare is itself an experimental concept that, if fruitful, will require new doctrine and retraining of commanders, staffs and the forces expected to execute these operations.

In addition, network centric doctrine may eventually have an impact on peace operations. It has the potential to link force elements in ways not now possible, but will by the same token require degrees of cooperability that are not now needed. The U.S. is also writing doctrine that facilitates network centric operations when dealing with non-NATO militaries, NGO's, PVO's,

---

[20] Sometimes referred to as the Scandinavian school.

[21] For a discussion of European views of Joint Vision 2010, the U.S. conceptual template for future military operations, read Michael Codner, "Joint Vision 2010 as a Conceptual Basis for Coalition Warfare and Operations of the Future", Appendix F.

IO's, and host governments, and will have to harmonize this doctrine with that of potential coalition members.

An emerging major doctrinal difference is the degree to which countries stress force protection when operating in support of coalition objectives. While all major powers are willing to accept casualties in direct defense of their homeland and major national interests, much less harmony exists in other operations, including marginal force-on-force operations as well as MOOTW. For the U.S. in particular, force protection has become a fundamental tenet. This has a very direct impact on operations as well as on research, development, and acquisition. Increasing reliance on stand-off weapons, stress on remote sensing and on massing sensors rather than weapons platforms, emphasis on avoiding casualties from friendly fire, on controlling the night, and on stealth technologies are all reflections of this tenet.

The Bosnia operation has highlighted the importance of this difference. Even today, with the threat of combat substantially reduced, U.S. forces move in their sector of Bosnia in well armed, multi-vehicle convoys. Moreover, U.S. forces stay largely in their compounds and wear protective gear (flak vests, helmets, etc.) whenever they are in an exposed location. The French and UK forces in Bosnia have much looser security unless under some heightened security posture. Their troops move in single vehicles and are not required to wear their protective equipment on routine moves. They are typically off the base and mingling with the population in their off-duty hours. French and UK commanders believe that their approach is both much more reassuring to the local population and also enables them to establish better communications with that population, thus having the opportunity to head off potential problems.

Information sharing is another arena where doctrines differ with profound consequences. The situation in Somalia, where the U.S. sent in a special intelligence element that worked only for U.S. commanders and shared intelligence only after it was sanitized, has already been mentioned. In general, coalition members have opted for an approach that assumes all information, whether about friendly forces, the adversary, or the operating environment, should be reviewed and controlled centrally. However, nations use very different approaches about what can and will be shared, with whom, and when.

Yet, as the technology chapter of this report points out, the increasing pace of events in military operations, as well as the increasing need for integrated activities that enable coalitions to take advantage of the full capabilities of the partners involved, make it essential that a relevant common operational picture be established and maintained. An outdated operational picture, or one that differs among the coalition partners, is very likely to engender uncoordinated, potentially counterproductive actions by different

Doctrine and Concept Development

elements of the coalition. Eventually, common doctrine can be expected to be a major contributor to establishing and maintaining a relevant common operational picture.

Organizational issues with implications for doctrine were discussed in chapter five. These include the distribution of authority and responsibility, the degree of centralization in the system as envisaged by the level of detail at which directives are published,[22] and the roles that the different commanders and units play in the chain of command. The degree to which a commander is permitted to ignore doctrine can also vary among nations. The old Soviet system demanded that officers exercise "initiative", but defined that as vigorous execution of the orders received from superiors rather than in the Western sense of the term, which implies creativity in the way the general goals of the superior commander are supported.

One aspect of doctrine that NATO has made progress in harmonizing is in the crucial function of logistics, with the ratification of *Allied Joint Publication 4, Logistics*, in 1999. This effort built on decades of NATO Cold War work considered essential to the defense of Western Europe against a Soviet attack, as well as on experience in Bosnia. Differences in logistics can have a profound impact on military operations. Hence, doctrine designed for operations with non-NATO coalition partners needs to include the dimension of logistics harmonization.

Doctrinal harmonization has also become increasingly important in the conduct of relations with the news media, particularly in peace operations. Some potential adversaries have sought to hide their misdeeds by excluding the press from their areas of operations. Democracies with traditions of press freedom have a need to keep the media informed, but differ widely in the mechanisms they use, and the degree of access granted. Failure to harmonize doctrine in this increasingly crucial arena where both military effectiveness and policy effectiveness are often determined, will lead to continuing problems at the strategic, operational, and tactical levels. Commenting on the public information aspects of IFOR operations in Bosnia, Pascale Siegel noted:

> National systems of operation were a source of recurring problems as different PI (public information) doctrines and procedures led to misinterpretations, incomprehension (sic), and difficulties among IFOR PI staff. From observations in the field, it seems that each

---

[22] Directives may be mission oriented, objective focused, or be presented as detailed orders indicating precisely what to do, when and where. For the four nations represented in this study, the doctrinal shift is in favor of a mission oriented approach. This is not true of a large number of potential coalition partners, particularly those coming from the Soviet doctrinal tradition or who are heavily dependent on conscript forces.

PIO (public information officer) was working at least as much with his national doctrine as with OPLAN 40105, ACE directives, of NATO doctrine.[23]

HOW TO HARMONIZE DOCTRINE

Getting agreed coalition doctrine is difficult for two reasons. Doctrine development is typically a painstaking process even at the national level, since it requires determining what works best in the view of military leaders based on recent experience and perceived future threats. In the past, common doctrine has been negotiated before it is agree. This has taken time.

As a result, it will be most practical for nations to agree on as many parameters as possible regarding collective military responses to threats. An approach to accomplish this is to use experimentation, with participation by actual and potential coalition members, as a way to achieve a common understanding of threats and collective responses. Writing of doctrine can then be expedited based on this common understanding. Threats and responses could be prioritized and generally agreed responses in the abstract of any specific geography, time, or scenario, but would still generate a type of military response that defines a common doctrinal need.

Written Allied joint doctrine in the NATO environment is still in its formative stages. As of the publication of this report, only a few documents have been published. That being said, it remains the best example to date of doctrinal cooperability and interoperability. A continuing challenge is that the process established to write NATO allied joint doctrine through the use of AJP's is cumbersome and lengthy. However, in spite of this challenge, the NATO allied joint doctrine process has potential application as a model that could be used by other allies when operating in coalition environments requiring a doctrinal construct.

In the future, when anticipating the use of military forces in a coalition operation, a doctrinal base for these operations should be established early in the planning process. Allied joint doctrine should be used whenever possible.

NATO offers an important example of how to harmonize doctrine. NATO military doctrine is developed by NATO member nations participating in the Military Agency for Standardization (MAS). MAS is a military agency under the Military Committee (MC) established in 1951 and charged with responsibility for developing "operational, procedural, and material standardization among member nations". The military director of MAS

---

[23] Pascale Combelles Siegel, *Target Bosnia: Integrating Information Activities in Peace Operations: NATO-led Operations in Bosnia-Herzegovina December 1995-1997* (Washington, DC: National Defense University, 1998).

Doctrine and Concept Development

reports to the Chairman of the Military Committee (CMC). Representatives of NATO's Strategic Commands (SC's) and Integrated Military Staff also participate in Working Group (WG) sessions under the MAS and provide discretionary advice, but they do not vote. Doctrine is agreed by a "majority" vote of eight nations - a number that was set prior to NATO enlargement and that may change in the future.

Until recently, doctrine has been developed under MAS by Army, Navy and Air Force Service Boards and promulgated as Allied Technical Publications (ATP's). In 1994, the Allied Joint Services Board was established in order to address joint services needs. The Joint Services Board's principal subordinate WG is the Allied Joint Operations Doctrine WG (AJOD-WG). The concept is for the AJOD-WG to be the primary developer of Allied Joint Doctrine, although the Service Boards will continue to develop combined service-specific doctrine for some time to come. AJP's are the new name for agreed allied doctrine. Thus far, only two AJP's have been approved: the 1997 capstone AJP-01 (Allied Joint Doctrine) and the 1999 AJP-4 (Allied Joint Logistics). Several others are under development: AJP-3 (Operations), a Netherlands lead project; AJP-3.4 (MOOTW), a U.S. lead project; and AJP-3.4.1 (Peace Support Operations) a UK lead project.

It is likely that a considerable number of ATP's will be re-issued as AJP's over time. Many older ATP's were validated recently during Balkan operations. The SC's may also develop doctrine or procedural publications. However, they should follow the principles of harmonizing doctrines through national authorities. The MC issues doctrine-related documents, such as MC 327 (Peace Support Operations), but these establish only broad policy upon which doctrine must then be developed. An intrinsic NATO problem is that its many member nations must work on and ultimately agree to a single doctrinal product. This guarantees a lengthy doctrine development and approval cycle.

Notwithstanding this constraint, NATO has established an extensive library of doctrinal publications, including some for coalition operations. Furthermore, when NATO has been required to execute missions for which there are considerable doctrinal voids, such as the 1995 IFOR mission, military commanders have quickly worked out agreed procedures and modified them as experience required. For all the Balkan missions, lessons learned have been collected through a Joint Analysis Team (JAT) and fed back into the doctrine development process.

In order to operate effectively during fast moving coalition operations, the doctrines of potential coalition partners must be harmonized in advance to the maximum extent possible. Doctrine is pervasive across all manner of military activity, and it is also in constant flux as new missions emerge, optimum methods are improved, and best practices are refined. Therefore harmonization of doctrine must be a constant activity.

Coalition Military Operations: The Way Ahead Through Cooperability

There are several evolutionary routes to harmonizing doctrine. The experience of operating together constitutes one, as does the use of exchange posts in national staffs and centers of doctrinal development and military education. Doctrinal development within NATO is an important focus of this activity. However, this incremental activity, essential though it is, by its nature will require considerable time to address the full range of coalition activities comprehensively, and is likely to lag behind the pace of technological change and alterations to the security environment. Furthermore, NATO's purview remains limited to the immediate proximity of the NATO area. In any event a normal method by which NATO makes progress has been and will be for one or more nations who have a concern to take forward work that is subsequently presented to NATO for consideration, amendment and eventual incorporation into the NATO corpus. The need to make coalition operations more effective and efficient is both immediate and continuing. Moreover, difficult issues such as information sharing, network centric operations, and media interactions have to be discussed among nations to enhance the NATO harmonization process.

As this study has concluded for other aspects of interoperability and cooperability, a series of well structured experiments in the form of simulations, war games, and field exercises is likely to be a most effective way of harmonizing doctrine. If each nation's key actors can take part in a series of experimental activities in a realistic set of situations, they will have the opportunity to confront and address the needs for interoperability and cooperability in a timely and cost effective way. Doctrinal differences that are subtle and all but invisible will come to the fore rapidly when commanders work together and forces seek to cooperate in generating relevant common operational pictures, collaborative plans, and integrated execution. Moreover, when these differences emerge in exercises, war games, simulations, and other types of experimental settings, the participants are both motivated to resolve them and positioned to document both the differences and how they were overcome.

However, harmonization remains too slow and cumbersome. Each nation comes to the process with more or less developed, yet often dissimilar doctrine for a particular operation. The process requires identification of whose doctrine works best. Often a hybrid doctrine is synthesized as a composite of several methods. Priorities are needed for the task of developing common doctrine. Potential partners need agreement on where doctrinal interoperability in coalition operations can afford the greatest improvements. Key areas to consider are command and control, deployment and sustainment tasks. The exercise of identifying doctrinal harmonization priorities will also yield information on weaknesses and outright gaps in coalition doctrine, as well as on salient disconnects among national doctrines. There is certain to be much to document in this area for future work.

FINDINGS

- Coalition operations in the recent past have required an ad hoc process of negotiation among the governments involved in order to establish broad command arrangements. The detailed command arrangements and the doctrine for the coalition have then been developed over time by the military participants in the coalition, also using an ad hoc process unique to each situation and set of participants.

- Some NATO doctrine and practice were designed for defensive allied operations in a Cold War environment and are not appropriate to current coalition operations. However, it is anticipated, based on efforts already underway, that NATO doctrine on allied operations, MOOTW, and peace support operations will be ratified in the short term.

- NATO is working on developing doctrine for Alliance members. However, that process does not seek to generate doctrine for coalitions involving nations outside NATO. Non-NATO nations need to be involved in some process to assure interoperability and cooperability.

- The NATO efforts now underway are striving to co-evolve ways to harmonize doctrine. The four nations represented in this working group should be aggressive in their support for NATO's efforts to increase the promulgation of Allied Joint Publications, and should also include doctrinal issues as part of the larger experimental program designed to ensure interoperability and cooperability in coalition operations.

- Harmonization of doctrine at high levels (above the national forces) is a key part of the discovery experiments needed to ensure smooth and effective coalition operations. The capability to harmonize military operations and efficiently to bridge national force efforts is a crucial measure of success.

- There are marked differences in the way that the four countries develop their military doctrines. Yet, each methodology aims to provide the doctrine necessary to meet the needs of similar operational concepts. Hence there is good reason to be optimistic about harmonizing doctrine if a concerted effort is made to do so.

- Significant issues of interoperability and cooperability will continue to be doctrinal. This is because doctrinal harmonization is all but essential at some level in order to be able to work together.

DEVELOPMENT OBJECTIVES

- The development of doctrine is but one part of putting together a mission capability package, and therefore must go hand in hand with the co-evolution of concepts of operation, organization, and supporting technological capabilities. Therefore, doctrinal considerations need to be an integral part of the previously recommended experimentation process to explore technologies and organizational forms.

- Doctrine needs to co-evolve in the experimentation process to achieve interoperability, cooperability, and seamless integration. An example of an approach to do this is a "thought experiment" that would imagine the future, its implications, and how the four countries deal with them. This thought experiment could take the form of a high-level wargame. In the U.S., these table top wargames involve role playing and scene setting. They are attended by very senior levels, with, for example, an under secretary of defense playing the secretary of defense, and are multi-department. In the context of this study, high level officials from just the four countries defense establishments would be involved. At the same time and in parallel, getting more allied operational military participation in exercises would be one way to bridge "echelons" and to create a feedback loop between the two levels and types of "experiments".

- Coalition doctrine development should be pursued within NATO, extending and modifying NATO's existing methods for doctrine development to encompass the specific capabilities attendant to coalition operations. However, NATO's process should speed up, with the goal of producing agreed doctrine within two years, if even on an interim basis. In order to generate new doctrine, NATO must adopt a markedly more flexible approach to current institutions, resource planning, exercise calendars and military guidance to nations.

- There needs to be emphasis and investment in extracting lessons learned from all coalition operations.

- There should be recognition of the roles of education, training, exercises, and exchange programs in doctrine development and refinement.

- Finally, the four nations participating in the study should collaborate more on national doctrine development with an eye toward harmonizing more fully both national and NATO doctrine. The resultant elements of a common doctrine should then form the basis for establishing training and exercise goals, and should be incorporated into coalition operations planning.

VII. CONCLUSIONS AND RECOMMENDATIONS

CONCLUSIONS

Historically, coalition military operations have been addressed through ad hoc processes of negotiations among the participating nations and non-governmental organizations. The organizational structure of the coalition, the detailed command arrangements, and the doctrine for the coalition have then been developed over time by the senior military participants in the coalition, also using an ad hoc process unique to each situation and set of participants. Ad hoc development even extends to special procedures dictated by the lack of technical interoperability between coalition partners.

Despite these difficulties, most coalition military operations have proven more or less successful. Yet, there have been a few spectacular failures as well as measured successes that came perilously close to failure. Even when deficiencies in the ability of coalition partners to operate together do not jeopardize mission success, they can result in unnecessary casualties in the field. This occurred, for example, in the 1991 Gulf War, when the lack of a common combat identification system among coalition members resulted in deaths from friendly fire. There is very clearly substantial room for improvement in the efficiency of coalition operations. Working group members believe that many opportunities now exist which, if seized, will allow future coalition partners to work together more effectively.

The cost of failing to do so may be extremely high. Coalition interventions are likely to face an increasingly difficult operating environment across the full range of missions considered in this study. Without improved coalition effectiveness, both mission success and the lives of military personnel will be at greater risk than they are today. Moreover, cooperability, meaning the degree to which the nations are willing to work together and to which concepts of operation, organization, and doctrine of coalition partners are compatible, is becoming more difficult to achieve. Yet, cooperability constitutes a critical factor in determining the efficiency of a coalition. Thus, in the absence of greater efforts, the political and operational effectiveness of coalitions will not simply stand still; it is rather likely to slide backwards.

Cooperability is becoming more difficult because of the different rates at which countries are adopting and assimilating new technologies, as well as of different cultural approaches that influence how militaries adapt their concepts of operation, organization, doctrine, education and training to exploit the new technological capabilities. The achievement of greater cooperability needs to build upon the promise of improved C^4ISR interoperability among coalition partners that advances in information technology offer. Most of the advances in information technology are products of the commercial sector and are widely available throughout the world. Developed for the mass market, information technology is more affordable than before. These factors make the application of advanced technology to the challenge of coalition technical interoperability more achievable even for severely restrained budgets.

Coalitions cannot operate effectively, or even be launched, if national risk assessments are too divergent. Decisive coalition action will depend on coalition partners reaching quick consensus on risk assessments. Each nation tends to assess the impact of future challenges through its own unique methodologies. The fact that future risks will spring from a growing diversity of national and transnational sources will make them even more unpredictable and difficult to characterize. Many decision-makers and planners do not fully understand adversarial thinking. The production of red team assessments could prove extremely useful in obtaining better insight regarding adversarial concepts, particularly in the use of asymmetric approaches. This would assist in providing a common as well as a comprehensive risk assessment. Much can be done in assessing risks that does not involve exchanges of classified information.

The study group believes that a very real need exists for a campaign of exploratory experimentation. In this campaign, promising approaches to coalition military operations would be subjected to the rigors of war games, simulations, command post exercises and other environments, such as the Combined Federated Battle Lab and Advanced Concept Technology Demonstrations, where they can be evaluated by coalition partners. Despite the "prevailing wisdom" that interoperability and cooperability are intangibles and cannot easily be measured or their impact on mission effectiveness ascertained, the working group believes that they are, in fact, excellent candidates for empirical analyses and for coordinated experimentation among allies and potential coalition partners.

Yet, formal hypothesis testing experimentation would require an unrealistic investment, and the realm of potential alternatives is simply too large to permit systematic examination of each one. Clearly, the problem calls for exploratory experimentation in which new approaches and alternatives are examined. Empirical observation and measurement will provide the ability to establish the value of these new approaches and to ensure that they have an impact on the key dimensions of decision-making quality, decision-making speed, and operational efficiency. Finally, an experimental campaign is needed because the problem is too complex to yield to a single experiment and because the best hope of good quality solutions arises from cumulative learning and knowledge.

Furthermore, undertaking a campaign of experimentation focused on coalition interoperability and cooperability would provide the participating governments, and the larger community of potential partners, with tangible measures and evidence of the benefits that can be expected from investments. In addition, taking advantage of existing laboratories, networks, and currently planned experiments would permit initiation of a broadened effort with little added infrastructure costs. Moreover, such a campaign will likely result in more efforts in this arena that build on the earlier work, and also to result in improved "real world" operations because the exercises will directly enhance both practical interoperability and the key human elements of cooperability. Each of the participating countries would contribute to defining the goals and specific experiments of the campaign.

From a technology standpoint, there are several areas related to threat assessment that the commercial sector cannot address to one degree or another. For example, little is known about how to model asymmetrical conflicts, thus hampering the threat assessment capability of all nations. Similarly, the relationship between technology and asymmetrical threats is only vaguely understood. Perhaps most importantly, the risks associated with technology and policy solutions to the problem of multi-level security need much more attention if coalitions are to operate most effectively. The study group believes that these areas are particularly appropriate for joint research among the nations represented in this study.

Finally, for most nations, coalition military operations as a functional area suffer from a lack of focus in the politico-military hierarchy. Responsibilities for technical interoperability and the various aspects of cooperability, where assigned at all, tend to be dispersed throughout a nation's security community, thus making it difficult for coalition partners to address issues of efficient operations in a focused way. Additionally, lessons learned from previous coalition operations tend to be narrowly drawn from the perspective of the responsible official's area of cognizance. Worse still, for lack of focus, lessons learned frequently evaporate upon reassignment of the individuals charged with drawing them in the first place. Clearly, a high level focus on coalition military operations in each nation's security structure would allow a greater concentration of effort in addressing means of enhancing military operations.

RECOMMENDATIONS

The recommendations below summarize the detailed development objectives found in each chapter, and they are applicable to all would-be coalition partners. Yet, it is the sense of the working group that the four nations represented in the study can, and should, form the nucleus through which the recommendations are implemented.

- Establish a multi-country analysis program on emerging security issues and establish data bases for the related contingencies. This program

would operate in confidentiality, using open sources and unclassified information. The program's output would be selectively available for publication. The program would include several coordinated activities:
- Assess the incorporation of extant and emerging technologies in asymmetric approaches to warfare.
- Modeling of asymmetrical conflicts.
- Develop a common methodology to assess the impact of threats and conduct analysis of alternative futures in the security environment as well as of their implications.
- Undertake analysis of adversary intentions, including the use of asymmetric means.
- Undertake a vulnerability assessment of current and potential coalitions.
- Highlight hot spots that may call for coalition operations in the future.

- Establish experimental programs to explore new concepts and technologies for the purpose of co-evolving common enhancements to coalition operations for peacekeeping, peace enforcement, and regional conflict. A cooperative process among the participating countries would define the goals and individual experiments of the program. The program would:
  - Take as a starting point current NATO experience and capitalize on existing laboratories, networks, research and planned experiments and exercises.
  - Incorporate other nations and non-governmental organizations as the experimental setting dictates.
  - Begin with a high-level, multi-national table top wargame that includes red/blue war-gaming and role playing by coalition participants.
  - Focus initially on shared awareness and efficient, coherent coalition planning and execution.
  - Explore risk management approaches to information sharing and security.

- Establish focal points in each nation to serve as the nation's focus for cooperability/ interoperability. The focal points would:
  - improve the development and writing of allied joint ***doctrine***.
  - improve the allied joint ***training*** system.
  - improve the allied joint professional military ***education*** system.
  - establish a cooperative coalition ***lessons learned*** activity.
  - improve cooperation for ***C^4ISR*** research, development and acquisition.

- improve the support for the use of open-system ***architectures*** and commercial ***standards*** in solving cooperability / interoperability requirements.
- evaluate new technology tools for improved crisis management and for addressing the risks of multi-level security.

APPENDIX A
ON DECISION-MAKING IN COALITION
Edouard Valensi

This presentation forms part of the informal discussions initiated by the U.S.-CREST under the quadripartite seminar "Coalition Military Operations and Warfare of the Future". It expands on an initial contribution "Designing a Defense Information Infrastructure for a Coalition: A Challenge". It offers a response to the question posed to the Technology Subgroup: "What research effort could be suggested to improve the decision-making process in coalition?"

Without making reference to any particular operation, nor seeking to concentrate on a given country, this essay describes the nature of the decisions taken, and identifies potential problem areas: the aim is to achieve timely agreement. On this basis, it suggests research areas which might offer improved working conditions for allied staffs on operations.

1. Engagement procedures, and hence staff work required, vary depending on the situation.

Figure 1 summarizes the type of organization taken as a model in the reference study: a coalition linked at staff level, whose units and weapon systems remain under national command and retain a direct link with national authorities.

It is at the decision-making level within a central staff HQ that the notion of coalition becomes a reality. The decision-making process collates the analysis and makes tangible the commitment of allied states to the action. To be effective this process is designed to be a confluence of national processes rather than their intersection. While ensuring that time is not wasted, the allies seek to take account of the approaches of each of the parties.

The dialogue process varies according to the type of conflict. Figure 2, which lists operations by classification, makes this self-evident. It is clear that between "operations in support of preventive diplomacy" and "a state of war", the tempo, diplomatic considerations and the nature of military operations differ radically.

General rules for engagement will be a function of the overall context of the military operation (conflict, crisis, etc.), and the framework of the commitment (national, multinational, inter-allied, UN mandated operation, etc). It is on the basis of the framework and national concepts for the use of

Coalition Military Operations: The Way Ahead Through Cooperability

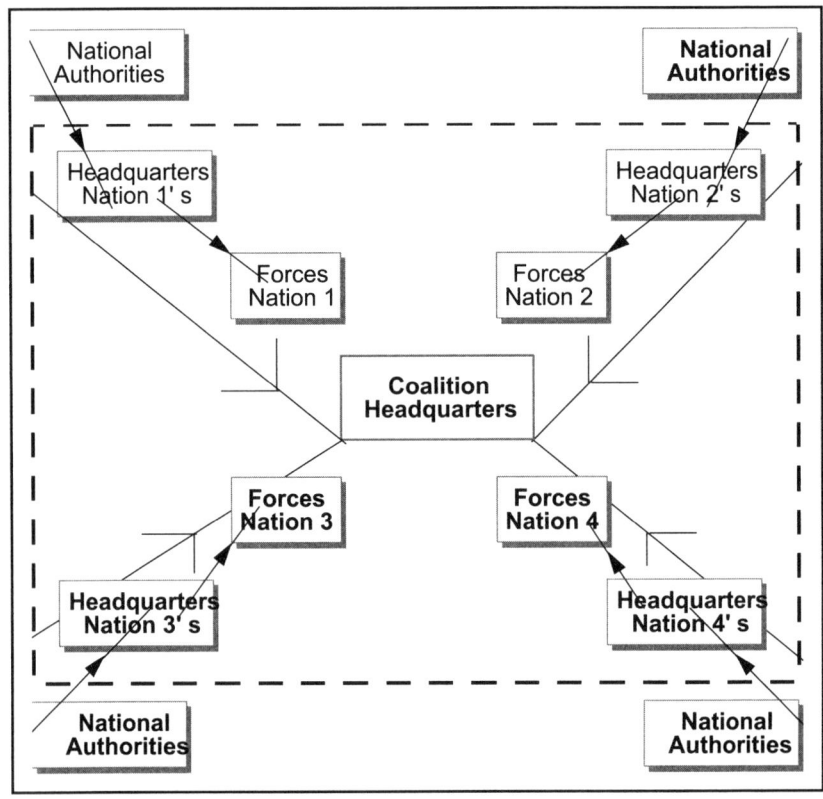

Figure 1

force that the crisis management process will be established. The crisis management process includes:

- starting from a political objective, and
- a desired end state (DES).

It will involve

- creating a military operation entitled the strategic option (task identification, type of engagement: projection of power or projection of forces),
- translating this action into a contingency or operational plan.

There are two distinct phases in planning for a military commitment:

- advance planning (*planification d'anticipation*) which terminates in the choice of an endorsed strategic option and a contingency plan, and

Appendix A

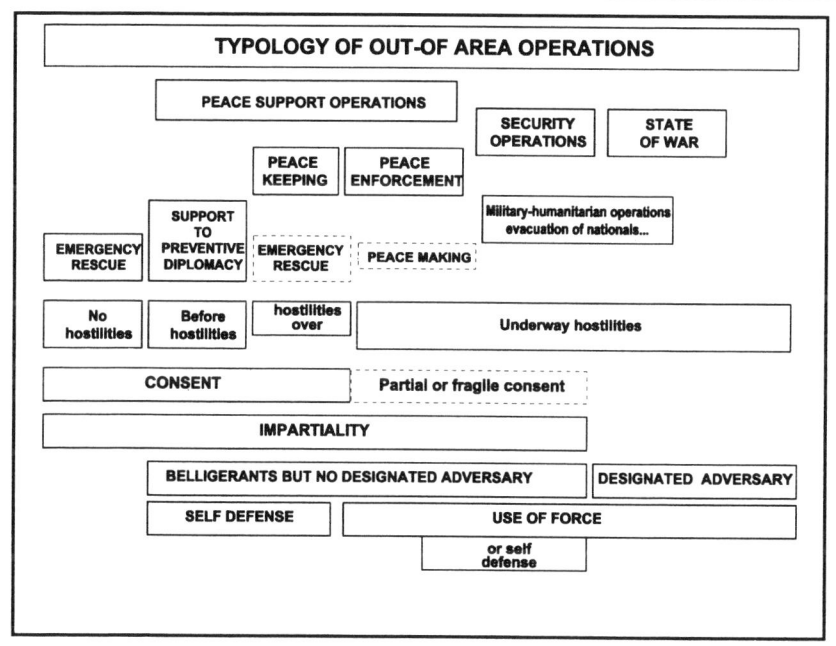

TYPOLOGY OF OUT-OF AREA OPERATIONS

	PEACE SUPPORT OPERATIONS			SECURITY OPERATIONS	STATE OF WAR
		PEACE KEEPING	PEACE ENFORCEMENT		
	SUPPORT TO PREVENTIVE DIPLOMACY	EMERGENCY RESCUE	PEACE MAKING	Military-humanitarian operations evacuation of nationals...	
EMERGENCY RESCUE					
No hostilities	Before hostilities	hostilities over	Underway hostilities		
CONSENT			Partial or fragile consent		
IMPARTIALITY					
BELLIGERANTS BUT NO DESIGNATED ADVERSARY				DESIGNATED ADVERSARY	
SELF DEFENSE		USE OF FORCE			
		or self defense			

Figure 2

- implementation planning (*planification de mise en œuvre*), which involves translating strategic options into operational plans.

Fundamentally, the decision-making processes of the partner nations in the coalition are very similar. This is shown in table 3 which reveals the close similarity between French procedures and those of NATO.

All the partners within a coalition agree to relate their military involvement to a political and diplomatic objective, which is also the grounds for their combined action. However, faced with the unexpected in crisis situations, differences in appreciation between coalition nations are inevitable. These are discussed during any major decision-making process.

2. Retaining national singularities

What emerged from discussions at meetings organized by U.S.-CREST was the fact that engagement without ulterior motives in coalition operations does not mean the abandonment of national singularities. This therefore is the assumption made here. Consequently our four nations' doctrines should be parallel. Such a comparison does not enters into DGA's missions. Nevertheless we need to refer to the French crisis management doctrine and Joint Pub.

PHASES	STAGES	Documents To Be Generated	NATO equivalence
Drafting of Initiating Directive		Initiating Directive	NAC's Initiating Directive
Orientation	Mission analysis Examination of the initiating directive Situation analysis Reformulation of the mission Presentation of conclusions Take account of CEMA comments Drafting	Strategic appreciation of the situation **Additional planning instructions**	Mission Analysis Review Identification Mission Statement Strategic Appreciation Briefing **MNC's Planning Guidance**
Identification of a Concept of Operations	Study of planning instructions Development of operational states Imagination Re-grouping Elimination Draft decision Confrontation, Comparison, Classification Decision taken by CEMA Drafting	Draft proposal **Concept of operations**	Planning Guidance Review COA's Development COA's Comparison Decision Briefing MNC's Concept of Operations
Development of Plan	Drafting Circulation Approval Distribution	**Contingency plan** Or **Operation plan**	Development Coordination Approval **MNC's Contingency Plan** or **MNC's Operation Plan**
Validation Update		**Contingency plan** Or **Operation plan** Update	Reviewed **MNC's Contingency Plan** or MNC's Operation Plan

Table 1

301, "Commander's Overview" that addresses mainly "Military Operations Other Than War" and Multinational Operations to outline what could be some research program. Both documents make reference to military decision-making sequences, which involve:

- a strategic cycle,
- a tactical cycle (72 to 96 hours), and
- an operational cycle (24 to 48 hours),

This must now include, for sensitive decisions of a political nature a dialogue involving national authorities. An additional sequence is therefore added to the preceding cycles:

- proposed decisions are formulated at theater level,
- these are discussed and endorsed by national authorities,
- and implemented on the ground.

The responsible authorities should be questioned to obtain a comprehensive view of discussions likely to take place between allies. While the strategic options are being established, discussions will take place to establish limits for the military action, and of course to define acceptable risk levels, especially for personnel. At the operational level, a major subject for discussion might be the balance to be struck between technology and man:

- Some consider that the "Revolution in Military Affairs", made possible by the explosion in advanced technology and formalized in the "Joint Vision 2010" project, is driving us towards ever more radical automation in the preparation and conduct of operations, and the allies of the U.S. are asked to join the integration process that this presupposes.

- For others, including European members of our group, Man must remain in control of the process. Therefore degrees of freedom must be maintained to ensure that the irreplaceable advantages offered by the presence of Man on the ground, his appreciation of the cultural environment and his situational intelligence remain the major factor behind the success of military operations. This means that there is always a certain independence in situational appreciation and a degree of initiative at implementation level.

3. Components of a research program

For the most part, future military operations will continue to be conducted in cooperation. It is therefore likely that the objective of "multilateral operations" will be cited in numerous programs and it will therefore signify little. Conversely, those responsible for cooperation may wish to push for the continuation of general technical programs (such as improving C^4ISR systems or bombardment capability).

However, there is no doubt that there is a problem specific to coalition operations. During discussion in the technology sub-group, it was stressed that decisions taken in coalition were complex, which leads to delay and a loss of sight of the objective. Here it was noted that: "coalition is not integration" and that the origin of the complexity in the decision-making process could lie in the need to take account of options seen as essential by allied nations, or differing analyses of the situation. Finally, it was recognized that the confrontation between methods and points of view that is made possible by co-operation between major allied service staffs enables significantly better decisions to be arrived at.

A research program into decision-making in coalition could give priority to techniques and resources, which would address the fundamental problem, by ensuring that under all circumstances an appropriate momentum was sustained during collective decision-making processes. Such a program would be all the more welcome as, during coalition operations, complex decision-making structures involving the interweaving of internal and external decision cycles must be retained. A joint program on decision-making in coalition could therefore be defined along these lines:

- It should refer back to current structures, in other words to the command architectures that enable service staffs to cooperate while remaining linked to their central national authorities.
- The study's ultimate aim should be to improve the dialogue process, reduce the time needed to take decisions and synchronize national activities.
- Account must be taken of allied nations' doctrines and rules of engagement, especially the reservations some may have concerning excessively constrained or automated decision-making procedures, that minimize opportunities for initiative by the combatants.

In this context it might be possible to take as a basis for discussion the acquisition of the functional capabilities needed to attain "information superiority". These capabilities have been examined in particular in Chapter III "Information Systems Technology" in the DoD's Defense Technology Area Plan. By concentrating on themes directly associated with decision-making in coalition, it should be possible to adopt the following subjects:

- Collaborative situation assessment, (ensure that coalition commanders have dominant battlespace knowledge),

Appendix A

- Common understanding and representation of the battlespace, i.e.: common operational picture (elevate the level of our cognitive understanding of the enemy, friendly, and geospatial situation; maintain consistency in that view across tactical and supporting forces),
- Shared, distributed collaborative planning, (going from manually intensive development of plans to partial then quasi-automated planning),
- Support of simultaneous, coordinated operations, (control of "coherent" coalition operations to optimized dynamic use of resources without preempting "intuitive" use),
- Knowledge-based access, retrieval and integration of information, and
- Automated translation (one of the most important challenges).

Programming of these studies must take account of the wide range of actions initiated on these subjects, especially within NATO working groups.

APPENDIX B
EXTENDING NETWORK-CENTRIC WARFARE TO COALITION CRISIS MANAGEMENT AND ASSESSMENT[1]

Dennis M. Gormley and Douglas M. Hart

The Context and Challenge

Discussions of network-centric warfare focus exclusively on the post-crisis phases of the conflict spectrum. Joint Vision 2010, the U.S. military's vision of an unfolding Revolution in Military Affairs, is no exception. But if there is any area where network-centric concepts and improved NATO interoperability could make a palpable difference, it is in the pre-crisis and crisis management phases of potential conflict. Decisive coalition action depends on disparate allies reaching quick consensus on threat perceptions. Future threats will spring from a growing diversity of sources (national and transnational) and will be ever more unpredictable and difficult to characterize.[2] And given the increasing probability that weapons of mass destruction will play a featured role as future threats, the consequences of threat misperception and crisis mismanagement will correspondingly grow.

In his threat paper prepared for our first meeting in Washington, Major General Alain Faupin wisely drew attention to the shortcomings in inter-allied threat perception and analysis reflected in virtually all post-cold war conflicts.[3] In trying to understand why so many of these conflicts remain inconclusive, Gen. Faupin argued that either we had a good perception and analysis of the threat but failed to tackle the challenge adequately, or we had partial knowledge of the threat and found success impossible to achieve no matter how good or ample the military resources applied to the conflict. Faupin's belief is that we have never had a thorough perception and analysis of the threat. Obviously political and cultural idiosyncrasies among its large membership will always make consensus on threats difficult within NATO or any large coalition of the willing. Yet the emergence of ever more

---

[1] This paper is adapted from a longer version that the authors prepared for a working group meeting at the Royal United Services Institute for Defence Studies, 19-21 October 1999. The full version can be found on the U.S.-CREST web site, at www.uscrest.org/CMO.htm.

[2] Transnational or non-state actor threats are unarguably difficult to characterize, but even traditional weapon system threats emanating from state actors have become equally challenging to monitor. See, for example, Dennis M. Gormley, "Hedging Against the Cruise-Missile Threat", Survival, Spring 1998, pp. 92-111.

[3] Major General Alain Faupin, "Threats: What's Up?" Prepared for the working group meeting of 17-19 March 1999, Washington, D.C., 17-19 March 1999. See U.S.-CREST web site.

ambiguous threats compels NATO to find ways to exploit new information technology to radically improve its crisis assessment and collaboration capabilities.

The concept of network-centric warfare (NCW) involves generating information advantage and turning it into competitive advantage. By netting together various users, high levels of shared battle-space awareness and collaboration about prospective military plans and operations can be achieved. This potentially speeds up decision-making for various battlefield missions like precision engagement, force protection, and dominant maneuver. But such networking has no less important a role to play in crisis assessment. Clearly, U.S. national technical means, battlefield surveillance sensors, and near-real time exploitation systems dominate the intelligence collection mission within NATO. However, NATO's European members seek some means of independent assessment, not least to avoid crisis assessment domination by the United States, but also to begin the long development process fundamental to a European Security and Defense Identity.

Although the United States currently dominates the intelligence collection side of crisis assessment and, as such, can share as much or as little of its information with its allies as security constraints permit, developments in the commercial satellite industry augur some interesting possibilities for future NATO collaboration. The failure of Franco-German partnering on the Helios 2 and Horus satellite programs has led to both countries investigating alternative paths to meeting their requirements. A broader partnering in the development of so-called cheap satellites might offer affordable choices on both sides of the Atlantic. Precisely such partnering has been championed by John Deutch, during his tenure as Director of Central Intelligence in 1996. Moreover, a recent solicitation by the Defense Advanced Research Projects Agency (DARPA) for the Discoverer II radar surveillance system encouraged bidders to consider European industrial partners. Broader government-to-government arrangements along the lines of collaboration found in the Joint Strike Fighter program are at least conceivable in the future development of space imaging systems.

But even before such collaboration in intelligence collection might take place, there is even more compelling reason for coalition partnership in the commercially driven technologies of data dissemination, fusion, and collaborative planning and execution. These areas are particularly germane to improved crisis management and assessment. Most important, the ongoing partnering among commercial information and communications industries across the Atlantic furnishes opportunities for America's European partners

Appendix B

to have a substantial industrial stake in any collaborative efforts that might apply NCW to crisis management and assessment[4].

Non-traditional or emergent threats demand new ways of fostering rapid, well-coordinated crisis options. By their very nature transnational and asymmetric threats require multi-partner solutions. New data mining techniques and assessment methodologies offer tools to help predict early signs of crisis emergence. New information technologies can be exploited to rapidly form crisis action teams within the alliance, providing team members in widely disparate locations seamless access to relevant data and shared consultations. New information assurance techniques can also help create needed barriers to protect certain sensitive categories of information. This paper elaborates the notion that NCW concepts and new information technologies can help foster greatly improved coalition crisis management and collaboration capabilities to meet the challenges of a more diverse and growing number of traditional and emergent threats to alliance interests.

Adapting to Changes in the Threat Environment

The end of the Cold War and the information technology revolution are transforming the threat environment. Smaller organizations are becoming more lethal while the threat environment is becoming more ambiguous. Small groups are more lethal in an absolute sense due to the breakdown in control over weapons of mass destruction and the growing traffic in delivery means. More importantly, small groups are relatively more lethal because, as they master the network organizational form, they can combine in unexpected and non-repetitive ways to threaten highly vulnerable elements of modern economies and civil societies. The increasing level of resources the United States is spending on infrastructure protection is evidence of a growing respect for such asymmetric threats.

It is increasingly clear, however, that hardening infrastructure (both physical and information) cannot provide the degree of protection sought by Western nations. The increasing strength that networks derive from information technology is serving to enhance the lethality and ambiguity associated with even the traditional end of the threat spectrum. The more NATO can dominate a local battle space, the more state and non-state adversaries will seek to carry the fight to NATO's homeland. Intelligent and adaptive adversaries will form networks with transnational organizations to acquire advanced weaponry, its means of delivery, and access to vulnerable

---

[4] European information technology industries are becoming increasingly competitive with their U.S. counterparts. According to the Gartner Group, European network integration and support services are expected to grow to more than $37.5 billion by 2001 at a compound annual rate of 12.5 percent

Coalition Military Operations: The Way Ahead Through Cooperability

NATO civil and military infrastructure. Given that the advantages lie with threat entities in the end game, the place to perceive threats and counter them is in crisis space when nascent threat networks are vulnerable to disruption. While battle space is dominated by operational military considerations, crisis space is far more heterogeneous and complex involving the full economic, political, religious, and ecological dimensions of the international security environment. Crises that precede or accompany Major Theater Wars, Peacekeeping/Disaster Relief Operations, National Evacuation Operations, and Anti-Terrorism Operations are all composed of an admixture of these elements. This is even more the case with respect to emergent threats. Transnational criminal organizations, cyber-terrorists, non-state ethnic/religious groups, etc. may possess aims that may either not be fundamentally military (e.g., the use of violence as a means for increasing profit), or may change over time as the network evolves (e.g., hackers may work for nation state intelligence organizations today and sell their services to narco-terrorists tomorrow).

NATO's member nations possess impressive resources that could be employed to map, navigate, and exploit crisis space to safeguard its collective economies and societies, but these assets are currently used piece meal on traditional diplomatic or military venues. NATO must possess the ability to rapidly form analytical communities of interest that can anticipate and keep pace with emerging crises while safeguarding unique intelligence sources and methods from compromise. Closer collaboration between the intelligence organizations of various NATO states suggests also that such collaboration extend to law enforcement communities of various partner states. Since threat entities from hostile states to transnational criminal organizations are making common cause and forming networks, it is imperative that NATO recast the definition of security to allow the free flow of vital information between the intelligence and law enforcement communities. Finally, because the information dimensions of crisis space are so daunting, and the data collection capabilities of NATO's constituents so (potentially) capable, maximum use must be made of information technology in order to derive warning, plan collaboratively, and act collectively as early in a crisis as possible.

New Information Technology Tools for Crisis Management

In order to face threats that can damage core NATO economic and societal infrastructures, however, NATO must develop more appropriate crisis management mechanisms that can operate continuously in crisis space. Taking just one example from discussions of the Threat/Mission Subgroup in Paris, NATO needs to improve its threat assessment capability. Not only do threat assessments take an inordinate amount of time to complete, but they are also watered down and disaggregated in their makeup. If sufficient political will can be mustered to fashion changes along the lines of much greater information sharing, there is new technology available to adapt readily to emerging threat challenges.

The information technology required to exploit crisis space can be grouped into the four basic categories:

- Online Analytical Processing (OLAP): An outgrowth of commercial data base technology, OLAP supports complex analysis in multi-dimensional environments. Analysts can rapidly navigate complex information spaces to confirm or deny hypotheses.
- Knowledge Discovery: Next generation search engine technology that is just entering the commercial market will allow analysts to generate and focus queries against large data sets with a much richer contextual background than current commercial, key word-based search engines. Applications based on techniques such as latent semantic processing and citation indexing will enable a sophisticated, interactive knowledge discovery process in which analysts identify new and previously unknown concepts and network relationships that can be tested using OLAP-based tools.
- Structured Argumentation and Evidential Reasoning: Argumentation tools, employing a template of hierarchical questions, can evaluate evidence in order to capture the analytical reasoning process from evidence to conclusions. Various approaches are used to manage both the uncertainties of the evidential data and the inference process itself. Argument templates focus analysis by leading users to drill-down hyperlinks, suggesting related questions to answer, and exposing information gaps.
- Corporate Memory: Commercial data warehousing technology provides persistent storage with vertically integrated software tools that enable comparison of critical information across situations, time, and organizations. The next generation of this technology will provide automated support for comparing current situations to known past crises to support collaborative crisis management.

These four information technology areas are currently being integrated into a crisis management environment under the auspices of DARPA's Project Genoa.[5] The goal is to develop a collaborative virtual environment that encourages rapid and efficient interaction by ad hoc and formal groupings at the analytical and policy-maker levels throughout the U.S.

---

[5] For more on DARPA's Project Genoa, including a White Paper, see http://dtsn.darpa.mil/ISO/infoexploit.asp.

national security community. The Genoa environment provides tools for organizing and analyzing masses of unstructured qualitative data gathered from diverse heterogeneous sources. Genoa also creates the means for capturing relevant data, logic and actions into a corporate memory, for generating options by policy-makers with drill down and exposure of rationale, and for building customizable, interactive, object-linked briefings with real-time data links.

The Genoa project is composed of four segments:

- CrisisNet: a computer network infrastructure that leverages internet concepts to provide a set of virtual enterprise services. These services could enable policy-makers and analysts to collaborate in a secure, integrated manner.
- CrisisBrowse: a versatile multimedia browser with uniform access to heterogeneous multimedia data. It provides information management through information organization, information push, and advanced visualization.
- CrisisBrief: enables policy-makers and analysts to organize and present information more intelligently, and provides a mechanism for policy-makers to provide feedback to analysts.
- CrisisScope: furnishes analytical tools for tracking on-going and evolving situations by collecting analysis arguments with corresponding evidence. Applications enable users to discover previously unknown critical data relationships. Argument templates capture the logic for crisis and policy option analysis and serve as a corporate memory for comparing and contrasting current analyses with the past.

Crisis Net, Browse, and Brief constitute Project Genoa's infrastructure and are essentially adaptations of commercial off-the-shelf information technology. CrisisScope involves applied research and development that focuses on analytical tools.[6] Both analysts and decision-makers conceivably would use these tools for intelligence and policy option assessments. CrisisScope addresses key issues associated with navigating crisis space. First is the need to identify relevant information from large volumes of data. Second is the ability to analyze these data to recognize a possible crisis and to provide the supporting evidence used to arrive at a conclusion. CrisisScope must be capable of generating evidence of a crisis amidst an overwhelming quantity of irrelevant, uncertain, and conflicting data. It must also be able to recognize impending crises early in their life cycle and be able to project

---

[6] Mark Lazaroff, *Project Genoa CrisisScope: Technical Report 1, Findings and Recommendations of the Research,* Pacific-Sierra Research, 30 April 1998.

mitigation actions. DARPA's goal is to develop a system that can provide a long-term corporate memory for crisis detection, analysis, and mitigation.

Genoa seeks to implement a rational human-computer division of labor. Analysts would be doing most of the thinking with information technology handling the collection, manipulation, and presentation of data. In Crisis-Scope, the goal is to provide analysts with tools to focus attention, bolster knowledge discovery, and support decisions enabling crisis warning, monitoring, and management.

All of the evidential reasoning tools described above require organized data to work efficiently. It is often said that analysts are drowning in data, but starving for information. Because the amount of information stored in unstructured text databases is increasing rapidly, it is becoming more difficult to locate relevant information in a humanly reasonable amount of time. On-line newspapers, books, corporate and government publications, and internal documents are growing in size rapidly, fueled by tremendous increases in computer speed and capacity. Most of this information is written in plain prose, and very little of it is formatted in easily searchable structured-relational databases.

Although current search technologies (e.g., key word and topic lists used in search engines such as AltaVista) provide access to large quantities of unstructured data, they tend to suffer from low precision. Under these conditions, the analyst will usually have to look through a large number of documents before finding the ones of interest. Project Genoa addresses these problems by providing powerful tools for navigating through the information in free text databases. Relevance feedback techniques, where the analyst supervises the search and retrieval process, help to cut through irrelevant information, and help to find important isolated information, which is discarded by traditional statistical-based search engines.

Toward Genuine Coalition Crisis Interoperability: The Role of Information Policy Management

In order to achieve the potential crisis management leverage associated with Project Genoa, its analytical product must be made available to all coalition members in near real-time. Recent advances in information technology can enable rapid dissemination of information across a coalition, but its integration into NATO must be accompanied by the development and implementation of a modern information policy. A coalition information policy must go far beyond traditional intelligence sharing relationships, which are rarely articulated rigorously and often implemented subjectively. A modern information policy begins with exhaustive analyses of mission-specific information and communications requirements. Given certain mission parameters, what information is available to individual members of the coalition and what bandwidth is required to distribute it with minimal latency to all the members? This foundational analysis can then be employed to build a series of mission-specific information policy matrixes containing information sources and coalition members. Each basic mission matrix will also have an associated series of excursion matrixes that anticipate information needs against worst case or likely deviations from the basic mission matrix.

The keys to the technical side of implementing a coalition information policy are gateway and data base technologies which will allow NATO to develop automated boundary controllers for sending and receiving data across command echelons, security systems, and national boundaries. Previously, enforcing information dissemination policy was a slow and manpower intensive process because it required visual inspection of product content. New commercial information technology, however, enables automated extraction of meta-data (product content description) from information products. One such software product produces both external meta-data (type, date, and format), and parses text data to discover internal meta-data (content, themes, and links to other documents/media).[7] Technical solutions are no longer the barrier. What is required is the political will to forge a modern information policy.

The Way Ahead

This paper has argued that the concept of network-centric warfare, which has focused exclusively on the application of military force, has an equally important role to play in assessing and managing crises. Ideally, the more effective prospective coalitions assess and manage crises, the less likely they will need to apply force.

Recent history illustrates the potential value of improved crisis collaboration within NATO. During the Persian Gulf War of 1990-91, the U.S. government essentially placed its crisis management agencies on a war footing by adding significant additional staffing dedicated to the monitoring and collaboration challenge. Moreover, U.S. interagency crisis managers collaborated closely with their European counterparts. As a result, the operations of about 30 terrorist squads of Iraqi origin were successfully identified, tracked, and foiled.[8]

---

[7] "Understanding the Oracle8I, an Oracle File System (iFS) Option", *Features Overview*, February 1999, pp. 4-5.

[8] See K. Scott McMahon. "Unconventional Nuclear, Biological, and Chemical Weapons Delivery Methods: Whither the 'Smuggled Bomb'", *Comparative Strategy*. 15:2 (Apr.-Jun. 1996), pp. 123-134.

Appendix B

Yet, once the level of accelerated preparedness dropped off after the Gulf War, a determined terrorist group managed to bomb the World Trade Center in February 1993. The Trade Center bombing succeeded not just because the U.S. Government "stood down" from its heightened crisis status during the Gulf War. Nevertheless, fewer eyes and decidedly less collaboration surely represent contributing factors. Although technology could never entirely replace accelerated human involvement in crisis management and collaboration, new information technologies such as Project Genoa do offer the prospect of significantly improving steady-state pre-crisis assessment and crisis management without corresponding increases in manpower.

The common feature of many of the technologies discussed here is that they contribute to a much greater understanding of what is occurring in diverse areas around the globe. While new collaborative technologies will not eliminate the increasingly opaque monitoring environments facing coalition governments, they do augur unprecedented pre-crisis and crisis transparency, making it easier for allies to form coalitions before aggression begins. In an era of growing uncertainty, that is surely an objective worthy of allied attention.

APPENDIX C
EXPERIMENTATION TYPOLOGY
Richard E. Hayes

Background

The term "experiment" has become a major "buzz word" in the Department of Defense over the past two years. Activities that would have been termed assessments, evaluations, proofs of concept, tests, demonstrations, and even exercises in past years are suddenly categorized as experiments. This development has been encouraged by reform-oriented members of the national security community, including influential members of Congress, who are concerned that the United States military may be lulled into a false sense of security by the absence of peer force threats. This concern is particularly high during an era when weapons of mass destruction and new technologies (particularly information technologies) create revolutionary opportunities for transforming warfare and the key arenas command and control, from sensing and fusion through decision making and battle management.

Experimentation has become seen as good within DoD because it is associated with science and new technologies, but also because, in the words of senior officers, experimentation allows, even benefits from, failure. Classic military exercises cannot be allowed to fail because they have an important role in training and because their failure reflects badly on the participating commanders and staffs, with potential career implications. Tests, assessments, and evaluations; particularly those focused on new systems and equipment, cannot be allowed to fail because they represent the culmination of lengthy and expensive research and development programs, and because their failure also has implications for the responsible people and organizations. Demonstrations are efforts to showcase new technologies and systems, so their failure defeats their purpose. Moreover, technology demonstrations have increasingly become a route around complex and cumbersome formal test and evaluation programs that are expected to leave behind systems improve that military capability in the field. By contrast, experimentation is seen as a legitimate "voyage of discovery" and a relatively systematic way to explore new approaches and the potential of new systems. Hence, experiments are seen as relatively risk free for both organizations and individuals and therefore attractive both to innovators and the military organizations asked to accept the risks associated with innovation.

Types of Experiments

Relatively few of those embracing the concept of experimentation within the Department of Defense have paid serious attention to the underlying concept. In fact, the term arises form the Latin, *experiri*, to try. Experimental knowledge differs from other knowledge in that it is always founded upon experience and observation. In other words, experiments are always empirical. A formal definition of experiment is, "A test made to demonstrate a known truth, to examine the validity of an hypothesis, or to determine the efficacy of something previously untried." Indeed, all three of these meanings are relevant to DoD experimental activities in the recent past and planned for the future. Moreover, these three groups correctly distinguish the three major roles that DoD organizations have assigned to experimentation:

- Hypothesis generation experiments involve providing new systems and technologies in a setting where their use can be observed and catalogued. The idea is to simultaneously find out if the innovation is useful (enhances military capability) and how it can be employed. This application is similar to the old process in which new military hardware (aircraft, tanks, etc.) were developed against a set of technical specifications (fly faster, fly higher, turn faster, etc.), then given to a technical user community (the Army's boards, Air Force test organizations) where the tactics, techniques and procedures for effective employment could be worked out. In these applications, the goal is to identify apparent military benefits and develop systematic theories about the best way the new technology or system can be employed, which includes specifying the conditions under which it can be used (and their limits) as well as the results that can be expected. The results of these efforts were "theories" in that they were not considered validated until the weapons systems had been turned over to end users (fighting forces) and employed under field conditions. Similarly, hypothesis generation experiments usually occur early in the development cycle and will not normally provide enough information (or evidence) to conclude that the observed relationship is valid or will occur reliably. Hence, they will normally be followed by other experimentation and related activities designed to refine the knowledge gained and provide added reliability and validity.

- Hypothesis testing experiments are analogous to the classic efforts of scholars to advance knowledge by seeking to falsify specific hypotheses (if...then statements), whole theories (systems of related hypotheses that "explain" some area of inquiry or domain of knowledge), or observable hypotheses deduced from such a theory. These empirical experiments are efforts to build knowledge. That is, the experimenter(s) create a situation in which one or more factor(s) of interest (at the data level, dependent variables) can be observed systematically (measured) under conditions that vary the values of factors thought to cause change (independent variables) in the factor(s) of interest, while other potentially relevant factors (control variables) are held constant, either empirically or through statistical manipulation. Hence, experimental results in science are always caveated with ceteris paribus, or "all other things being equal." Since the numbers of causal factors and dependent variables of interest in the military arena are both very large, a great deal of hypothesis testing experimentation is implied when military innovation is attempted. Considerable thought and effort will be required to plan sound experimental programs, both to ensure that individual experiments generate useful results and to ensure that large programs are designed to accumulate knowledge systematically and effectively across multiple experiments.

- Demonstration of known truth is analogous to experiments conducted in high school and college laboratories, where the students follow instructions that allow them to demonstrate, for themselves, that the laws of chemistry and physics operate as the underlying theories predict. These are similar to the technology demonstrations that have become significant within DoD in the past several years. However, the key difference is that demonstrations conducted as part of an experimental program will require systematic data collection in order to document the impact of new systems and technologies. Hence, they quantify the results that demonstrate the expected impacts while, at the same time, both validating the earlier research and experimentation and helping to establish a baseline against which the impact of future innovations can be measured.

All three types of experimentation have already taken place within DoD and are part of the overall planning for future experimentation at the Service and Joint levels. Hence, they properly belong to different parts of the research, development, and innovation process. Hypothesis generation experiments should ideally be conducted when the uses and limits of innovations intended to create new military capabilities are being explored. They should both provide indications of the potential utility of the innovation and also help to identify the best way(s) to employ them and the non-technological changes (doctrine, staffing, training, etc.) needed to permit full benefit from the innovation. Hypothesis testing experiments explore the dynamics of the innovation and the changes it enables or forces in the dynamics of the C^2 process. They are about cause and effect and establishing valid and reliable knowledge about the uses, limits, unintended consequences, and benefits available from the innovation. The bulk of experimental effort should, in an ideal DoD program, be spent on these hypothesis testing efforts. Demonstration experiments should occur only when the dynamics and benefits of a particular innovation (or set of related innovations) have been established.

Their primary purpose is to demonstrate the efficacy of the innovation to the user or operational community. They will differ from technical demonstrations only in the rigor with which they are observed and the benefits from the innovation are measured. This rigor, however, is important in that it provides the kind of evidence that can guide budgetary decisions and establishes performance baselines against which future innovation can be measured. For some parts of the user community, but by no means all, this empirical evidence will help to establish the credibility of the innovation.

Given that these three types of experimentation have somewhat different objectives and roles within the DoD research, development, and acquisition processes, they should be managed somewhat differently. For example, the product of hypothesis generation experimentation should be a set of hypotheses which are considered important to explore further, but do not stand as established knowledge. Hence, they will often be conducted with less rigor (and therefore lower costs) and across a broader range of contexts than the other two types. Hypothesis testing experiments, by contrast, require somewhat greater control and should yield structured data, information, and knowledge. Moreover, the complexity of establishing cause and effect relationships with enough rigor to support investment decisions will require both designs that create layers of experimentation (mini-experiments inside experiments, experiments inside mega-experiments, linkages over time across sets of experiments) and also provide for sampling of the experimental space in ways that allow credible inference across the range of important military threats, missions, and operating environments.

However, innovation within the Department of Defense is not a scientific endeavor with the luxury of infinite time to develop new knowledge. Information technologies are changing at an incredible rate. Adversaries have the potential to leapfrog generations of systems and technologies and can be anticipated to adapt commercial innovations to military applications. Moreover, the number and variety of opportunities to conduct experiments, particularly outside the training exercises which must use existing doctrine, organizations, and personnel, will continue to be modest. Hence, DoD's experimentation program will sometimes mix the three types of experimentation. In its simplest form, this may involve efforts to collapse the process by merging hypothesis generation and hypothesis testing experiments. A more complex variation may involve using hypothesis testing experiments on one system or technology to provide the context for hypothesis generation experiments on different innovations. While such combinations are certainly possible, they must be conducted carefully to ensure that each effort generates valid and reliable results to the research issues. Failure to keep the different goals and products well in hand will almost certainly lead to ambiguous results and the need for costly repetitions.

Coalition Experimentation

Coalition experimentation involves a variety of novel challenges not inherent in national efforts. First, information security becomes paramount. Every participating nation must agree to support the effort and to protect the research results from publication and from disclosure in forums where they can be misused. For example, coalition experimentation that identifies specific weaknesses in the C^{4}ISR system is valuable to coalition partners because it will help them make improvements. However, the same information can be exploited by adversaries. Moreover, publicity about weaknesses can be exploited by opponents of national governments for political purposes.

Second, coalitions are, by definition, made up of militaries with different traditions and philosophies. Hence, they will not start with the same view of how C^{4}ISR systems should be assessed or what the proper metrics are for a particular experiment. Hence, time and effort must be devoted to developing a common language, a common set of perceptions about the issues to be addressed, and an agreed approach to measurement. Even the way the experiments are to be reported may be a source of confusion and discussion. Hence, provision must be made for appropriate experts from all the participating countries to work together to design the experiments.

Third, burden sharing is an issue in any coalition activity, including experimentation. The sites to be used, the experimentation team, the equipment to be used, the subjects involved, and all items related to costs and burdens will need to be negotiated. This implies the existence of a high level steering group empowered to commit each of the participating nations.

Finally, coalition experimentation requires appropriate channels for review and release of results in each of the participating nations. This acts as a guarantee to the participants that they can ensure the results are interpreted intelligently and in the appropriate context.

APPENDIX D
POTENTIAL COALITION EXPERIMENTS
Richard E. Hayes

BACKGROUND

The US Joint C^{4}ISR Battle Laboratory (JBC) has made contact with several close coalition partners and begun discussions of a Combined Federated Battle Laboratory structure that would be available for coalition experimentation. Their approach is informed by the perceived success of recent JWID's and the associated coalition wide area network (CWAN). Discussions to date have focused on infrastructure - where the sites will be located in the participating countries, how long haul connectivity will be established and maintained, who will pay for which parts of the infrastructure, etc. These efforts appear to be bearing fruit and a system capable of initial experimentation is being established with the active support of NATO and US geographic CINC's. Because of the charter of the JBC and the other organizations involved, interoperability issues will be the first priority for these efforts. However, this is understood to imply support for the development of policy, doctrine, and procedures that underlie successful coalition operations. Nations actively involved and planning to support CBFL sites now include U.S. (including all military services), UK, NATO (including SHAPE), Canada, Australia, and New Zealand.

APPLICATIONS

As currently envisioned and under discussion, the first application is likely to involve the ability to formulate, communicate, and digest a theater wide Air Tasking Order (ATO), including new "non-traditional" coalition partners. This will also include moving the same information among military services for the forces in the coalition as well as informing the ATO's from a common operational picture (COP). Ideally, this will be supported on very small systems - down to the size of a personal computer. A larger scale effort also under discussion would link UK (DERA) Master Battle Planner with the USAF's Theater Battle Management Core System (TBMCS).

The CBFL initiative may also represent an opportunity for coalition experimentation that addresses key issues. For example, the ability to create and maintain shared awareness of the battlespace has been identified as potentially very valuable for coalition operations. The obvious idea that coalition partners looking at different information may generate different perceptions of the situation, which would cause them to either reach different conclusions about the correct course of action or take actions that are uncoordinated and inefficient provides the rationale for hypothesis generation and analysis. However, the very practical issues of what information coalition partners will be willing and able to share as well as the more cognitive issue of whether shared awareness will be adequate to improve force coordination and efficiency will also require systematic investigation.

These propositions could be organized into an experimental campaign that would (a) allow willing coalition partners to expand and improve their data and information sharing with a goal to establishing greater shared awareness, while at the same time (b) exploring the linkage between greater shared awareness and more effective and efficient C^{4}ISR performance and force effectiveness. Such a campaign could be organized so that the efforts move from very simple experiments that emphasize better connectivity and more shared data and information to more complex command post exercises in which the impact of better connectivity and more data and information sharing are examined in simulated environments.

BENEFITS

Taking advantage of the CBFL initiative would have several immediate benefits. First, it would make some interoperability experiments readily available with little additional infrastructure costs. Second, it has the potential to increase the number and variety of participants in the CBFL, thus strengthening that initiative. Third, it would immediately allow constructive and authoritative determination of what data and information can and should be shared by coalition partners, helping to make future plans realistic. Fourth, it would allow the coalition partners to address the issue of how information and data from different sources and different nations can be integrated in order to create shared awareness. Fifth, it would establish the legitimacy of an "experimental" approach that will permit generating answers to technical issues within a context informed by the full range of important doctrinal, organizational, and mission issues. Finally, it would allow meaningful examination of the benefits and limits of key elements of emerging approaches such as network centric warfare in the context of the sets of missions and threats that can be foreseen.

APPENDIX E
COMPLEXITY
Uwe Wiemken

From the beginning information technologies have caused confidence problems for the users. Defining an information technology system as some kind of model with some input and some outputs, a major problem is the question whether the system is reliable. If the system represents a physical model that may mean that it describes an experiment correctly, and if it represents a software business toll that may mean that it meets exactly the specifications of the customer (and has no hidden properties). Within very few years the complexity of such systems (hardware and software) has increased extremely fast thus leaving the domains where we have an intuitive awareness of the problem and the possible solutions. It may for instance be difficult to realize an input fault because we cannot connect directly the given result to the input. Even when we have access to the source codes it may be practically impossible to analyze such a model completely.

There are basically two ways to build up confidence for such systems. One is the formal and interactive or automated proof of logical consistency. It is possible to prove that an algorithm, which calculates the square of any number in a given domain, is logically consistent and correct. There is a lot of research going on to apply formal automated methods to verify software in this sense or at least identify suspicious parts but to date only rather small systems can be analyzed adequately.

The other method of building confidence is simply empirical. Taking the model as a mathematically formulated model of physical reality we have a long-term experience (since the beginning of the seventeenth century that is) with building up confidence to the level where there is no reasonable doubt any more. The process is driven by carefully planned experiments designed to verify or falsify the model. This is the backbone of our western industrialized societies. The process is extremely "conservative" meaning that the scientific community is very careful in accepting something new (e.g. a new particle), it is very slow compared to market driven developments but on the other hand it is extremely reliable.

Transferring this process to the domain of IT systems designed to "organize and support" and finally automates flows of actions etc. we must accept that we cannot base our assessment on such good "reliability measures" as in classic science. Having a decision-maker in the loop, an experiment may well be irreproducible and we usually don't have enough time to do as many experiments as might be desirable. In addition to hardly avoidable programming faults we even cannot exclude that a builder of such a system has implemented "hidden" functions which serve as hidden purposes. And if the support functions of such a system are relevant for individual or even national survival as in the military domain we need very high confidence before we are willing to rely on them. We need "measures and reliability".

To our knowledge little work is done to analyze this basic problem. We therefore would suggest to initiate studies addressing (among others) the following problems:

- What is the status of automated formal proving methods and what role can then play in the confidence building process in coalition operations?
- Is it possible to identify programming faults or hidden functions automatically or to support the search for instance by presenting program structure elements graphically?
- Can a graphic representation of model outputs help to support plausibility (like the finite element methods in the past)?
- Is it possible or likely that the civilian market adequately solves interoperability problems, especially the "hidden function problem"?
- How is the problem of reproducibility affected by the use of soft computing methods like fuzzy logic or neural networks?
- Is it possible to agree on any measures of reliability between coalition partners?
- Can the process be improved by means of automated testing or partly automated simulation with the decision-maker in the loop?

APPENDIX F
JOINT VISION 2010 AS A CONCEPTUAL BASIS FOR COALITION WARFARE AND OPERATIONS OF THE FUTURE
Michael Codner

The issue of interoperability among potential partners in coalition operations has been one of concern in recent years. A rather dry but adequate definition of interoperability is "the ability of systems, units or forces to provide services to and accept services from other systems, units or forces and to use these services so exchanged to enable them to operate effectively together".[1] Interoperability is, of course, not an end in itself. The incontrovertible aim of interoperability "to enhance operational effectiveness and improve efficiency in the use of available resources".[2]

At the top of the hierarchy of interoperability are national institutional prescriptions and guidance in the form of government policy and national military strategy. These are influenced by national constitutions, law and custom. They in turn influence and are influenced by military doctrine and informal behavioral relations within and among armed forces. National policy and national military strategy also govern investment in research and development and expenditure on new military capabilities and other resources for defense. Differences between nations in their national military strategic concepts will therefore have profound implications for interoperability in all its dimensions, organizational, behavioral and technical.

So some congruence or harmonization of nations' military strategic concepts is essential if there is to be progress in the matter of coalition interoperability. There must be some agreement not only as to the sorts of missions in which the forces of coalition partners might take part in the future but also as to how military force will be used. If there is no common view as to the answer to the "how" question, interoperability becomes little more than a matter of establishing connectivity between forces of different nations so that information can be shared. Matters such as maximizing the use of that information and maximizing the efficiency of multinational formations go out of the window. Also any degree of real integration below the operational level becomes extremely difficult. Those nations who achieve a degree of strategic congruence will be able to achieve higher levels of interoperability in all its forms than those who do not - other considerations being equal.

---

[1] Allied Joint Publication 1.

[2] Allied Joint Publication 1.

Coalition Military Operations: The Way Ahead Through Cooperability

Of the major military powers within NATO only the United States in its Joint Vision 2010 (JV2010) has published a clear military strategic concept for the longer term. The United Kingdom has recently completed its Strategic Defense Review. The White Paper that presented the conclusions addressed the longer term risks to security fairly adequately in the first chapter. But there was something of a step change from the long term to the near to medium term thereafter. Germany is in the middle of its own review and it remains to be seen how the result will address the longer term. One suspects that France has no more of a coherent vision for the longer term than Britain. None of these the nations have published the equivalent of JV2010.

When we turn to NATO we find a new strategic concept. This is of course grand strategy and we await the subordinate "military implementation" document but there are in the text very few "hooks" for a robust military concept there to deal even with the short term. There is mention of NATO's involvement in operations beyond those associated with Article V and perhaps further afield than the Article VI area but nothing for instance about the role of emergent technology. To be fair the Defense Capabilities Initiative that was published at the same time as the New Strategic Concept goes some way to confronting short term capability shortcomings. But there is certainly none of the coherent prescriptive guidance for new capabilities that could be drawn from NATO's Cold War strategic concept of forward defense and flexible response and its subordinate papers.

So it behooves the European powers to give careful attention to JV 2010 first and foremost because it is the only concept on the table. Secondly, of course, the U.S. is more or less committed to this concept. As we expect at least for much of the time to have the U.S. as a major partner in future coalition operations, we need to decide to what extent we are going along the same route as they and to what extent we, individually or severally as nations, are not. And if we are not, then where are we going individually or together on our separate ways.

There is another problem. Nations may have defense policy for the future - and a military strategic concept is part of defense policy insofar as it includes high level objectives and choices that are endorsed by government - but they do not have future defense policy. Yet however the security environment evolves, one thing is certain and that is that the defense policies of all nations will change. Furthermore defense policies are the result of today's political compromises. That is part of the democratic process. Yet it is defense policy as it is today that drives defense programs and provides the funding for them. Future capabilities are based on today's perception of future needs such as they are - a perception based on compromise which is grounded in itself on differing political perceptions. And this is why today's European perceptions of JV 2010 are very important to improving interoperability in the longer term.

Appendix F

It is not possible in this short paper to describe JV 2010 with adequate justice and the text of the unclassified version is widely available. Indeed it is not clear that everyone understands the same things from this concept defined as it is by such tenets as information superiority leading via dominant manoeuver, precision strike, focused logistics and full dimensional protection, to full spectrum dominance. Even within official defense circles in the U.S. perceptions vary widely. JV2010 is formally described as a "conceptual template". At one extreme some see its value as essentially experimental. But if one judges by its wide use in Pentagon presentations, then clearly for many it is the prolegomenon to every future operational concept of the U.S. military.

One might remark in passing for the benefit those not familiar with military doctrine that the middle four tenets of JV2010, manoeuver, strike, protection and logistics, are generally accepted as principal combat functions. And what nation's military would not want these to be as good as possible, namely: dominant, precise, comprehensive and focused? They are nonetheless combat functions. However figuratively expressions such as manouevre and strike are used by soldiers as tenets of, say, peace support or humanitarian operations, one gets the impression that this is primarily a "conceptual template" for sustained combat at high levels of violence.

JV 2010 can be crudely described as follows:

- It is about force projection and power projection. It is about conducting operations at considerable distance from the homeland in which combat is threatened or used. If the Czech Republic does not have plans to do this, it is not for them. The UK and France share this aspiration. Will Germany after its Review?
- It is global in its vision and requirements for reach. Do European nations have the same requirements of their forces? One suspects that the UK sees the Gulf as far enough for force planning purposes.
- It intends to make use of leading edge technology, particularly information technology for two principal reasons: first, because it is important to maintain technological advantage over possible opponents for its own sake. Secondly it is only through technology that the efficiencies can be achieved to counter rising equipment costs and the shortages in manpower and its expense. Other nations may not be so concerned over technological advantage but should certainly consider the efficiency arguments seriously.
- By the same token successful implementation is dependent on a high level of research and development and therefore of money up front.
- Furthermore, it is an experimental concept. Many of the subordinate concepts such as digitization of the battlespace and network centric

warfare are evolving and entail technological risk. They may not work as envisaged.
- As suggested earlier it is first and foremost a concept that addresses the needs of high intensity conflict. It expects to make use of manoeuverist principles to achieve quick victory making maximum use of the effects of disruption and coercion.
- It requires investment in expensive equipment such as sophisticated sensors, precision munitions and stealth.

There are some frequently voiced European criticisms of JV 2010. They are important because they reveal differences in perceptions among nations and the political compromises that each nation must make. These views will not be found in this extreme form in official statements nor can they be ascribed one by one to any particular nation or government. They are deliberately expressed bluntly here because one needs to understand the limits of the argument. And these are in reverse order of offensiveness:

- Cost. This is clearly the major problem for many potential coalition partners - first in collaborating in research and development and secondly in purchasing systems exploiting leading edge technology.
- Legacy problems. Nations are saddled with old equipment that cannot be modified. Nor can they afford to replace it sufficiently rapidly to keep up with U.S. developments.
- Technological risk. Will it work or are we being sold a pig in a poke?
- Have the implications been fully thought through particularly in terms of de-layered organizational structures involving authority devolved to low levels of command in highly politically sensitive environments?
- Conversely, is there a conflict in network centric warfare between the requirements to produce synchronized effect and the avowed emphasis on mission style command and initiative?
- How relevant is the concept to the most likely scenarios of peace support and humanitarian operations where disruption is an inappropriate concept and coercion will only be used occasionally in tightly controlled circumstances? Indeed reassurance may be as important as coercion.
- Indeed, what relevance has a concept predicated on concentrating overwhelming violence to achieve decisive results on the more likely constabulary operations in which force is only used in minimum amounts and as a last resort in the enforcement of international law or a mandate?
- What Professor Paul Rogers calls "liddism". The emphasis on global power projection represents a U.S. disposition to use the military instrument to put the lid on security problems rather than investing in

Appendix F

non-military means to resolve the underlying causes. Identification of rogue states and emphasis on counter-force solutions to the problems of weapons of mass destruction are evidence of this.

- Political hegemony. JV 2010 envisages a military system of systems of systems that you must either join or be left forever in the cold. If you join, you sacrifice national autonomy and freedom of action.
- Industrial dominance. If a nation cannot afford to be a major partner in collaborative development with the U.S., it will be forced to buy American. In particular military information technology will be sewn up in favor of U.S. solutions developed and marketed by U.S. companies.

This is a very mixed bag of very reasonable concerns and outrageous slurs but space does not permit a more measured presentation.

There are of course some equally forceful U.S. criticisms of European views. (It bears mention in passing that what really sticks in a British craw is the tendency to lump all Europeans together as equally delinquent in matters of responsible defense whereas the UK has been trying to hang on in there as the loyal junior partner spending well above the NATO European average on defense):

- There is a shortage of European investment in defense and in the military systems that will be essential for a secure future;
- There is a lack of global vision amongst Europeans, a lack of awareness of the vulnerability of Western security - in particular Western economies - to instability elsewhere through the effects of globalization;
- And these two criticisms come together under the broad heading of a lack of "burden sharing" and awareness of the need to support successive U.S. Administrations in their commitment in particular to European security by agreeing to support the wider security interests of the U.S.

So much for sniping across the Pond. In searching for a way ahead we need to acknowledge certain givens:

- European defense spending is not going to increase to anything like U.S. levels. The best greater European integration under ESDI might do is to create greater efficiencies and advantages of scale and to give more justification into sustaining existing levels. Under a number of measures the commitment of resources to defense of the European members of NATO is high by international standards and by a measure of potency developed by the Royal United Services Institute[3] France and Britain rank in the top five nations of the world after the U.S. and China - all permanent members of the Security Council. There are good reasons for the greater investment of the U.S. Among other things one might consider that there are thresholds above which extra spending really makes a difference. The U.S. is unique in getting a return for defense spending in the premier division. There is perhaps a first division that can get significant returns in terms of international influence that other nations represented here belong. But smaller European nations can see no significant return in support of national interest for greater defense spending.

- Europe faces some different security problems to the U.S. In particular the perimeter of the European Union is riddled with insecurities most of which are not amenable to military solutions. Even amongst the NATO nations there are variations in concern from the new members who are still predominantly concerned with territorial defense to Greece and Turkey with their mutual problems to some of the other southern nations and their concerns for the Mediterranean perimeter.
- We will need to accept degrees of interoperability even within NATO nations. It is not possible for all new members and some of the older members to achieve levels of integration in all environments comparable to those of some of the major and medium powers. Nevertheless, if we can achieve high levels of interoperability among a few significant nations, they in turn can be core or framework nations for other more modest military powers who may have other associations with those nations - for instance through the development of European formations. The same is true outside Europe with other groupings, for instance the Five Power Defense Arrangements,[4] the Pacific grouping involving the United States forces and the many bilateral relationships.

Some components of a way ahead for France, Germany, the UK and U.S., in the quest for interoperability are as follows:

- Develop a list of common missions defined by nature, relevance and intensity of combat activity and geographical scope as a substitute for a common strategic concept;
- As for the "how" element, avoid treating JV 2010 as a package but consider the applicability of its elements. Indeed avoid the label

---

[3] "The RUSI Index of Martial Potency" in *The RUSI International Security Review 2000*, London: RUSI, 1999.

[4] Among Australia, Malaysia, New Zealand, Singapore and the United Kingdom.

"JV2010" in multinational discussions of the requirements of multinational interoperability because of the baggage it brings;
- Emphasize the C^4ISR6 aspects of JV2010 as prior requirements for interoperability as these are a requirement for maximizing effectiveness in most types of mission;
- In particular acknowledge the significance of information superiority and of network centric activities as means of maximizing efficiency in the use of military force in the longer term. Work alongside the U.S. in the conceptual interpretation of implications;
- Accept the legacy problem and the need for incremental development of interoperable capabilities;
- Accept that European nations will be averse to technological risk and will to some extent want to "wait and see" for technology to mature;
- Use NATO as a repository if not a vehicle for progress in interoperability.

However, European nations:

- Need to strike a balance between collaboration with the U.S. in research and development and in buying mature technology off the shelf that will be cost-effective and preserve adequate autonomy;
- Have the opportunity to exploit the potential of ESDI to provide efficiencies and advantages of scale in the longer term

And finally Allied nations, including the U.S., need to resolve the issue of the relevance of high intensity combat capability to operations such as peace support. Traditional arguments will appear weaker and less sustainable in debates over balance of investment in the future. Of these the argument frequently used in UK is that high intensity combat capability designed for the less likely but more crucial missions in terms of national security and interest can be used for the more probable low intensity operations of choice but not vice versa.

A stronger argument is that it is high intensity combat capability that actually defines what military armed forces are and distinguishes them from other forms of organized force. If military forces do not bring with them evidence of the coercive edge that their high intensity capability gives them, they allow themselves to become victims of escalation and of perhaps the unlimited objectives of other parties in a complex emergency. The military forces of a nation that do not have this edge have a deficit in their ability to induce and will be dependent on the military forces of another nation that has maintained the coercive edge. In the Allied context this means that European nations that do not have this edge will sacrifice autonomy and freedom of action. Furthermore there will be the danger of inadvertent role specialization between the U.S. and European nations: the U.S. specializing in very violent highly coercive and disruptive short duration operations; the Europeans providing the gendarmerie on the ground for long-term messy complex emergencies. Few European nations would relish this prospect.

APPENDIX G
GLOSSARY OF SELECTED TERMS

Semantic Interoperability: The ability of a user to access, consistently and coherently, similar (though autonomously defined and managed) classes of digital objects and services distributed across heterogeneous repositories, with federating or mediating software compensating for site-by-site variations.
http://ai6.pbp.arizona.edu/tng/SemInterop/sld006.htm

Data Mining: A hot buzzword for a class of database applications that look for hidden patterns in a group of data. For example, data mining software can help retail companies find customers with common interests. The term is commonly misused to describe software that presents data in new ways. True data mining software doesn't just change the presentation, but actually discovers previously unknown relationships among the data.
http://www.pcwebopaedia.com/TERM/d/data_mining.html

Visualization: Visualization is the process of representing abstract business or scientific data as images that can aid in understanding the meaning of the data.
http://whatis.com/visualiz.htm

Collaboration Environment: Collaboration Environment is the capability for people with computers to work on a common area of interest either as a group or in a distributed way. The computers must have software that allows connectivity with all other group members. The software may include video, white boards, sound, and maps.

Multilevel security, or ***MLS***, is a capability that allows information with different sensitivities (i.e., classification and compartments) to be simultaneously stored and processed in an information system with users having different security clearances, authorizations, and needs to know, while preventing users from accessing information for which they are not cleared, do not have authorization, or do not have the need to know. MLS capabilities often can help overcome the operational constraints imposed by system-high operations and can foster more effective operations. For example, systems once separated by an airgap or connected only by a sneaker net may be electronically interconnected by an MLS guard, allowing the data transferred to be current rather than merely historical in value.
http://nsi.org/Library/Compsec/sec1.html

Common Operational Picture: Where commanders have or share the same understanding of the operation situation.

Advanced Technology Demonstration (ATD) *and Advanced Concept Technology Demonstrations (ACTD):* These develop, demonstrate, and evaluate emerging technologies and these activities precede the formal acquisition process. ***ATD's*** are typically integrated demonstrations that are conducted to demonstrate the feasibility and maturity of an emerging technology. http://www.acq.osd.mil

NATO C3 Interoperability Testing Infrastructure: The NATO C3 Interoperability Testing Infrastructure (NIETI) is an essential supporting element of the NATO C3 Interoperability Environment (NIE). NATO envisions a rigorous process of verification, validation, and test as systems are designed and implemented.

NATO C3 Interoperability Environment: an environment facilitating "the ability of systems, units, or forces to provide services to and accept services from other systems, units, and forces and to use these services so exchanged to enable them to operate effectively together".

Asymmetric Warfare: warfare that seeks to avoid an opponent's strengths: it is an approach that tries to focus whatever may be one side's comparative advantages against it's enemies relative weaknesses. In a way, seeking asymmetries is fundamental to all warfighting. But in the modern context, asymmetrical warfare emphasizes what are popularly perceived as unconventional or nontraditional methodologies. (Page 1, Challenging the United States Symmetrically and Asymmetrically: Can America be Defeated? Edited by Lloyd J. Matthews of the USAWC/SSI in 1998)

APPENDIX H
LIST OF WORKING GROUP MEMBERS

FRANCE
*IGA Bernard Besson, French MoD
Dr. Yves Boyer, FRS
*ADM Thierry d'Arbonneau, French MoD
Dr. Jean-François Delpech, U.S.-CREST
ADM François Dupont, French MoD
MG (ret) Alain Faupin, Marshall Center
BG Loup Francart, French MoD
IGA François Naville, French MoD
Dr. Xavier Pasco, FRS
CdV Bruno Sarrade, French MoD
IGA Paul-Ivan de Saint-Germain, FRS
IGA Édouard Valensi, French MoD

GERMANY
LTC Jens Clasen, German MoD
LTC Michael Coers, German MoD
COL Karl Heinz Drechsler, German MoD
*BG Ernst Lutz, German MoD
Joachim Rohde, SWP
Dr. K.- Peter Stratmann, SWP
*COL Reinhard Vogt, German MoD
LTC Helge Westphal, German MoD
Dr. Uwe Wiemken, Fraunhofer Institute

UNITED KINGDOM
*CAPT Simon Branch-Evans, British MoD
*RADM (ret) Richard Cobbold, RUSI
Michael Codner, RUSI
LTC Chris Collett, British MoD
Andy Nicholson, British MoD
Jeremy Stocker, RUSI

UNITED STATES
Dr. David S. Alberts, U.S. DoD
LTC David Anhalt, U.S. DoD
LTC Michelle Atchison, U.S. DoD
LTC (ret) Charles Barry, Barry Consulting

*Denotes member of the Senior Advisory Board

BG Richard Bundy, U.S. DoD
*MG George Close. U.S. DoD
Dr. Judith Daly, U.S. DoD
Barry DeRoze, U.S. DoD
*Joseph Eash, III, U.S. DoD
David Erickson, U.S. DoD
Christopher Fornecker, U.S. DoD
Dr. Richard Hayes, Evidence Based Research
Dr. Dennis Gormley, Blue Ridge Consulting
Dr. Robert Grant, U.S.-CREST
Kenneth Knight, U.S. DoD
Dr. Joe Luquire, U.S.-CREST
RADM (ret) Jim McFarland, Oracle
Dr. Spiros Pallas, U.S. DoD
Richard Radcliffe, U.S. DoD
Andrew Roberts, U.S. DoD
Dr. Michael Spirtas, U.S.-CREST
COL Tom Tyrrell, U.S. DoD

ABOUT THE FOUR INSTITUTES

U.S.-CREST

The **U.S.-Center for Research and Education on Strategy and Technology** is a private, non-profit public policy research institute incorporated in 1989. U.S.-CREST's central goal is to promote public understanding of the far-reaching interactions between transatlantic relations, defense, and science and technology.

FRS

The **Fondation pour la Recherche Stratégique** provides assessments of defense and security policies, of security-related technology issues, and of the sociology of conflict. The Fondation's work contributes to public policy decision-making, to the public debate in France on strategic and security issues, and to the diffusion of French thinking.

RUSI

Founded in 1831 by the Duke of Wellington and based in the center of Whitehall, London, the **Royal United Services Institute** is the oldest intitute of its kind in the world. It is a professional and independent authority dedicated to the study, analysis and debate of issues affecting defense and international security.

SWP

The **Stiftung Wissenschaft und Politik** is a foundation that was established in 1962 for the purpose of furthering analytical research into problems of international affairs. Publicly funded, but politically independent, the SWP today constitutes the largest research institute of its kind in the Federal Republic of Germany.